Eagles in the Dust

Eagles in the Dust

The Roman Defeat at Adrianople AD 378

Adrian Coombs-Hoar

Pen & Sword
MILITARY

First published in Great Britain in 2015 by
Pen & Sword Military
an imprint of
Pen & Sword Books Ltd
47 Church Street
Barnsley
South Yorkshire
S70 2AS

ISBN 978 1 78159 088 1

A CIP catalogue record for this book is available from the British
Library

Typeset in Ehrhardt by
Mac Style Ltd, Bridlington, East Yorkshire
Printed and bound in the UK by CPI Group (UK) Ltd,
Croydon, CRO 4YY

Pen & Sword Books Ltd incorporates the imprints of Pen & Sword
Archaeology, Atlas, Aviation, Battleground, Discovery, Family
History, History, Maritime, Military, Naval, Politics, Railways, Select,
Transport, True Crime, and Fiction, Frontline Books, Leo Cooper,
Praetorian Press, Seaforth Publishing and Wharncliffe.

For a complete list of Pen & Sword titles please contact
PEN & SWORD BOOKS LIMITED
47 Church Street, Barnsley, South Yorkshire, S70 2AS, England
E-mail: enquiries@pen-and-sword.co.uk
Website: www.pen-and-sword.co.uk

Contents

Maps & Diagrams

Acknowledgements

I would like to thank all those people who have inspired me to undertake this work, and also those who provided me with the encouragement and support to be able to complete it.

I would like to thank Pavel Simak for his excellent cover art 'Eagles in the Dust – The Fall of Valens'. I would also like to thank John Hills for supplying the map and diagrams plus his thoughtful comments.

I would like to thank Michael King Macdona for helping me with translations where needed, for his knowledge of the Battle of Adrianople, and for the many interesting conversations we have had in connection with the Late Roman Empire. I would also like to thank Francis Hagan for similar reasons and for the insights he has provided.

Further mention must be made to Chris Richards and David Mather for their comments and suggestions.

I would like to thank all those historians, academics and researchers whose invaluable work I have been able to consult during my own research for this book. And I would like to thank Ammianus Marcellinus for providing me with many hours of entertaining reading.

Due to the amount of material that is available concerning the Late Roman Empire, its army and its enemies, it would be difficult to give acknowledgment to all those whose works I have consulted and so I apologize to those who I have not done so.

Finally I would like to thank Ann for putting up with piles of books and papers lying around the house and for supplying me with endless cups of tea and other beverages upon demand!

To all those I have loved and lost

Introduction

The annals record no such massacre of a battle except the one at Cannae, although the Romans more than once, deceived by trickery due to an adverse breeze of Fortune, yielded for a time to ill-success in their wars, and although the storied dirges of the Greeks have mourned over many a contest.

So wrote Ammianus Marcellinus, Roman Tribune and historian who wrote one of the more graphic accounts of the Battle of Adrianopole.

At approximately 6.00 am on 9 August AD 378, a Roman army led by Valens, the Emperor of the Eastern Roman Empire, marched from the city of Adrianople to meet a Gothic army led by Fritigern, a Gothic Chieftain at a distance of between eight and twelve miles from that city. By 8.00 pm that evening two thirds of Valens' army lay dead or dying on the battlefield, including Valens himself who perished fighting alongside his army on that day.

This book not only examines that battle in depth, but also discusses the events leading up to it, the causes of the Roman and Gothic conflict leading up to the battle, and its aftermath. It will pose questions such as how Valens' war against the Goths may have been prevented, how the disaster at Adrianople may have been averted etc.

I will also discuss the Roman Empire's relationship with the Goths from when they first entered into the Roman histories up to the time of Valens' first campaigns against them and on to the battle and its immediate aftermath.

The most important ancient historical sources, several by those contemporary with the battle, have been included as have biographies of the main characters that featured before and during the battle.

I have also included a chapter concerning a number of 'what if' scenarios that may have changed not only the course of the battle but may ultimately have changed the course of history itself.

The completion of this book is culmination of thirty years' interest and research into not only the battle but the events leading up to the battle during the previous one hundred years. This was a time of transition for the Roman Empire, from when it almost fell during the Crisis of the third century, the rebuilding during the early to mid fourth century and then to the Empire having to make an accommodation with a 'barbarian' tribe that they could not eject from within their frontiers. The wealth of literary material concerning the Late Roman Empire that has appeared over the last fifteen years or so has been astounding, almost every month a new article or book appears discussing aspects of the Roman Empire that the time frame of this book covers. There were so many excellent works to choose from whilst carrying out research for this book that I must apologize if some of them do not get a mention.

By looking at the whole picture of the Romano/Gothic relationship I have chanced upon some aspects of this relationship that I believe have been overlooked and which had a bearing on the Battle of Adrianople. I will be discussing these and more in the relevant chapters.

Chapter One

The Goths

Their Origins, Tribal Structure, Home Life and Warlike Ability

The Goths, who were they and where did they come from?

If you were to ask the vast majority of people about 'Goths' they would more than likely tell you about those rather morose young people who have a penchant for wearing black, listening to sombre music and a strange fascination with vampires!

A much smaller number would probably remember something about some 'barbarians who sacked the city of Rome a long time ago'.

It is a sad reflection of these modern times that a group of peoples that had so much influence over European history have almost disappeared from the memory of those who live in those lands that felt their influence.

The origins of the Goths are still very much a matter of debate. The earliest surviving account of the origins of the Goths is that contained within *De Origine Actibusque Getarum*, better known as *The Origin and Deeds of the Goths*. Written in the AD '550s' by an Eastern Roman bureaucrat by the name of Jordanes, who himself claimed Gothic descent; it was an abbreviation of a much larger work, now sadly lost, by Cassiodorus. Jordanes stated that the Goths originated from 'Scandza', which was 'a great island situated in the surge of the northern Ocean', and that this 'island' was 'in the shape of a juniper leaf with bulging sides that taper down to a point at a long end'. The location of Scandza was in the Baltic Sea at the mouth of the Vistula River in northern Poland, putting it off the eastern coast of Sweden.

According to Jordanes, the Goths left Scandza in a fleet of boats under their king, Berig, and where they landed was then known afterwards as 'Gothiscandza'. This was in all likelihood in the vicinity of the area of northern Poland where the Vistula River flowed into the Baltic. Although

Jordanes' work no doubt contains much fantasy and myth, there is probably an element of truth in it; it's just dividing the fact from fiction that is the main problem. This area of Poland was the location of the Wielbark culture. This culture stretched south-eastwards, following the course of the Vistula until it encountered the Prezeworsk culture which stretched further south/south eastwards. It's believed that the expansion of the Wielbark culture into the Prezeworsk culture led to the creation of the Satana-de-Mures/Cernjachov culture further east around the region north and west of the Black Sea including the Danube, the Carpathians and the northern shore of the Black Sea itself. This version of the origin of the Goths is roughly that espoused by authors such as Wolfram (1990, 1997) and Heather (1991, 1998, and 2009), although not shared by all historians, notably Kulikowski (2009).

Gothic tribal structure was headed by the Iudex or King, like Athanaricus, or often just a very powerful or charismatic chieftain such as Fritigern. Beneath the ruler were the lesser but still powerful chieftains, such as Alavivus and Fritigern initially were, then the chieftain's retainers, then came the common peoples and then finally the slaves. Men were the dominant members of their society; the role of women appeared to be nothing more than to keep house and rear children.

The Goths themselves were broken up into a number of tribal groupings, each with a variety of names. However, by the fourth century the Goths were divided into two dominant tribal groupings, these were the Tervingi and the Greuthungi Goths. The transition from a number of Gothic tribal groupings to two larger dominant groups was probably as a result of several powerful Gothic leaders assimilating most of the other Gothic tribes through a series of military campaigns, as Jordanes' history suggests. The Tervingi were in the main settled around the area of the Carpathians whilst the Greuthungi lived in the more steppe-like area to the east of the Tervingi, roughly in the area to the north of the Caspian Sea. The main differences between the two tribal groupings appear to have been that the Tervingi warriors were mostly infantry, with a smaller number of cavalry formed by the richer nobles, whilst the Greuthungi appear to be mostly cavalry warriors with a smaller number of foot bowmen.[1] This is not an unreasonable view as the terrain both tribes were located in would have dictated the nature and style of their warfare, i.e. the more rough and hilly/mountainous terrain in the Carpathians was more conducive to warriors who fought on foot, whilst the more open steppes north of the Caspian Sea would have favoured mounted warfare.

There are very few indications of the style of clothing the Goths favoured. Their clothing did not appear to merit any real comment by contemporary historians. The best we can say is that the clothing would have been simple, probably tunic and long trousers for the men and a basic dress for the women. Clothing colour would have been natural colours, such as browns, greens and off-white.

Literary references coupled with grave finds indicate that at least before AD 376 most Gothic warriors would have been unarmoured, only the nobles, chieftains and kings would have worn body armour and helmets. The Tervingi infantry would have mostly been armed with a spear and shield, usually round or oval although some may have had a more 'traditional' hexagonal, almost coffin-shaped one. All the Goths would have had in addition a long knife, and some would have been armed with a bow, very similar to their Greuthungi counterparts. Swords would have been rare and before the crossing of the Danube in AD 376 only the kings, chieftains and nobles would have possessed them. The Tervingi noble cavalry, and the main bulk of the Greuthungi cavalry would likely have been mostly unarmoured and armed either with a long spear (*contus*), held with both hands or a pair of shorter spears that could be thrown as the later Goths were described as doing so by Procopius.[2] All the warriors, both foot and mounted, appeared to have worn a knee length tunic and long trousers that reached the ankles, with shoes as shown in pen and ink drawings of the now almost destroyed Column of Arcadius and the destroyed Column of Theodosius, both located in the Beyazit area of Istanbul.[3] However, by the time of the Battle of Adrianople itself it is highly likely that most of the Goths would have been almost as well equipped as their Roman counterparts, having had ample opportunity to strip the arms and armour from the bodies of the Romans killed or captured in the various skirmishes and battles between AD 376 and 378.

Both tribes formed mobile 'cities' made from the wagons they travelled in. Whilst no contemporary account exists that details exactly what these Gothic wagons looked like, there is a description in Ammianus that details the Alans, and their wagons. As the Alans' territory bordered that of the Greuthungi, it not unreasonable to assume their wagons would have been very similar to that of the Gothic ones. This is the description of the Alan wagons:

> For they have no huts and care nothing for using the plowshare, but they live upon flesh and an abundance of milk, and dwell in wagons, which they cover with rounded canopies of bark and drive over the boundless wastes. And when they come to a place rich in grass, they place their carts in a circle and feed like wild beasts. As soon as the fodder is used up, they place their cities, as we might call them, on the wagons and so convey them: in the wagons the males have intercourse with the women, and in the wagons their babes are born and reared: wagons form their permanent dwellings, and wherever they come, that place they look upon as their natural home. Driving their plow-cattle before them, they pasture them with their flocks, and they give particular attention to breeding horses.[4]

There is a contradiction in this passage in that whilst Ammianus indicates those using the wagons lived in them, and performed most human functions in them, he also stated that the Alans (and presumably the Goths as well) placed their 'cities' back on the wagons when they were ready to move on. This suggests that the bark wagon canopies could be placed on the ground and be used like tents, and then put back on the wagons when they were preparing to travel. This would be the natural thing to do as these canopies could then be the places where other family members or even slaves could sleep. Unfortunately Ammianus does not indicate what the draft animals used to pull the wagons were, but they could well have been the 'plow-cattle', i.e. oxen, he referred to.

The wagons themselves are a mystery, although it's fairly certain they had four wheels and were pulled by a team of animals, such wagons are shown in the pen and ink drawings of the Column of Arcadius and in a number of medieval manuscripts and artworks. The only sources we can really draw on concerning wagons and their contents in a similar situation to the Goths are those drawn from diaries and books written by travellers during the Great Migration period in the United States between 1840 and 1860. The wagons used by the migrants during that period were constructed from hard woods such as oak, poplar, ash etc. They had to be constructed as strongly as possible in order to survive the punishing conditions they were going to face. The bed or base of a typical wagon was 9 or 10ft long, 2ft wide with sides that were 2ft high. The width does not appear very wide at all but contemporary American records state that this was wide enough for the occupants to sleep in, even with the boxes in the base containing the tools and supplies needed for the journey (the occupants then sleeping on top of the boxes themselves). The boxes would contain food supplies, tools, cooking utensils, spare clothing, weapons, rope and a shovel. There would also be water kegs which could also be kept in hoops on the sides of the wagon. There was a single pole which the draft animals could be yoked to. These wagons were pulled either by a team of six horses/mules or a yoke of four oxen. The wagons could potentially carry as much as 6,000 pounds in weight but this was very extreme, the normal maximum was 2,500 pounds whilst the recommended maximum was 1,600 pounds. A surviving supply list for a family of four from this period had the wagon carrying 800 pounds of flour, 200 pounds of lard, 700 pounds of bacon, 200 pounds of beans, 100 pounds of fruit, 75 pounds of coffee and 25 pounds of salt. A Gothic list would have exchanged the bacon for mutton or horse flesh and of course no coffee![5] In 1847 a wagon train travelling to Oregon to California was composed of 1,336 males, 789 females, and 1,384 children of both sexes. They travelled in 941 wagons and took with them 469 sheep, 7,846 cattle, and 929 horses and mules.[6]

The preferred draft animals were either oxen or mules, oxen had the overall preference as they tended to be both cheaper to replace and also stronger than mules. Oxen were also more docile than mules, easy to work with, were less likely to be stolen and could exist on very sparse vegetation. The only problem they presented was when they were thirsty they could stampede towards the nearest visible water source.

The Goths would have had flocks of sheep on the journey and they would have been the animals that provided the wool for clothing, meat for the table and also the majority of the milk for drinking. The plow-cattle and horses taken along would also have supplied meat and also leather for shoes, belts etc.

We know from the American migrants' accounts that the average hourly rate of travel was approximately two miles an hour, and the average distance covered per day was just ten to twelve miles.[7] Only the elderly or small children rode in the wagons, everyone else either travelled on foot or on horseback. The wagons could be transported over very difficult terrain and across rivers and were in this way very versatile vehicles. They did suffer due to the nature of the terrain and the weather conditions; as a result wheel and pole breakages were fairly common.

Whilst applying the above to the Tervingi and Greuthungi, there is some evidence that the Tervingi Goths did have more permanent dwellings, and that at times they were even prepared to use disused Roman fortifications as a base, as will be discussed in Chapter Five.[8] The Tervingi who lived in more permanent dwellings probably grew simple crops of wheat and root vegetables.

So what made a Goth a 'Goth'? What was that something about the Goths that differentiated them from the other, similar tribal groupings beyond the Rhine and Danube? What made a Roman looking at a typical Goth know that it was a Goth they were looking at and not a member of the Alamannic tribe for example?

There are three main possible reasons why a person living in the Roman Empire during the fourth century would know he was looking at a Goth; these are appearance, clothing styles and language. Unfortunately the surviving histories that discuss the Goths tell us very little concrete about any of these three things. They do not describe in any detail the clothing the Goths wore, nor do they really indicate whether the Goths looked any different from the other tribes that the Romans were in contact with north of the Rhine/Danube during the fourth century. That just leaves language, which is probably the most noticeable difference people would use to determine if someone was culturally different from them. The Goths did indeed appear to have a language specific to themselves and remarkably, unlike practically all the other tribes north of the Danube/Rhine, who had an oral tradition, the Gothic language had a written form. The written form of Gothic was created specifically by Bishop Ulfila, who was himself a Goth. Ulfila had been ordained sometime in the AD '340s' during the reign of the Emperor Constantius II. This written form of Gothic was used to create a beautiful version of the Christian Bible, fragments of which survive and are now housed in the University Library of Uppsala in Sweden.[9] The importance of Christianity and of being seen to be Christian to the Goths will be discussed in Chapter Ten where the Goths under the command of Fritigern, having converted to Christianity, sent embassies to the Romans that were made up of Christian priests.

What were the Goths martial abilities? It is evident that the Goths were formidable opponents. The Goths, like the other tribes living north of the Danube and the Rhine, made raids into Roman territory. Unlike the other tribes these raids often took the form of full scale invasions, with the intention of remaining within the borders of the Roman Empire. The Goths appeared more than capable of raising extremely large numbers of warriors for campaigns across the Caspian Sea and the Danube, and these campaigns could last several years in duration. They managed to reach the walls of Rome and after the Battle of Adrianople they appeared more than willing to even make an attempt upon Constantinople itself. There are indications that the Goths used siege equipment on more than one occasion during the third century although they appear to have lacked this ability during the fourth century as they were unable to take walled cities like Adrianople and Constantinople as Ammianus noted (see Chapter Twelve).[10] The descriptions given by the Romans of the battles against the Goths are often written in such a way as to indicate their fighting prowess was, if not admired, at least respected. Their warriors were more than able to match their Roman counterparts on the battlefield and the danger for the Romans was that if their forces did not outnumber those of the Goths then they faced the very real danger of being defeated (see Chapter Eight). The Goths were also unusual in that they mounted naval attacks, although there is no record of any such attacks similar to those in the third century happening during the fourth century.

Looking at the Gothic experience of being forced from the lands they had once occupied, one can but imagine the terrors and dangers the Goths faced on their trek towards the perceived safety of the Roman Empire. They not only faced the fear of almost constant attacks by the Huns and Alans, who were hot on their tails, but also from other tribes along their route. Lack of food and water for both humans and their animals must also have been a grave concern, as was the fear of an outbreak of disease. These are exactly the kinds of things the American migrants spoke about in their diaries and journals. Deaths amongst the Gothic migrants could also have been potentially high. It has been calculated that a casualty rate of at least 4 per cent could be expected on the migrations across America. The highest cause of death was from disease, the next highest was from native American Indian attacks.[11]

The vast majority of those who have made a study of the Goths, and of the Battle of Adrianople, have not really assessed what it must have been like for them as a people driven from the lands they knew by a new and terrifying enemy. What must their thoughts and feelings have been and how must the complete dread of being slain by the invaders of their land have been for them to not only leave their lands, but seek sanctuary within the lands of a very powerful Empire, and one that was a potential enemy at that? Similar situations are happening even to this day, where people are forced to flee from where they live to cross over to other lands to seek sanctuary. Modern studies of forced migration and of the refugee experience, in journals such as *International Migration Review*, books by authors such as Agier (2008), and college/university courses offered by organizations such as the Refugees Study Centre, Oxford have looked at this very question and can give a very good insight into how the Goths must have felt and acted under such terrible circumstances.

Chapter Two

The Goths' Part in the
'Crisis of the Third Century'

And Roman-Gothic Relations Up To the Reign of Valens

Whoever the Goths were and where they actually originated from, we leave to future historians with the help of archaeologists to determine. The first attested raid by Gothic forces upon the Roman Empire was in AD 238 when the Goths attacked the city of Histria at the mouth of the Danube on the west coast of the Black Sea.[1] The sack of Histria led to the Romans paying the Goths to hand back those hostages they captured during the sack, and to leave Roman territory. Unfortunately the arrival of the Goths upon the frontier of the Roman Empire happened at exactly the same time as the 'Crisis of the Third Century', where the Roman Empire was assailed from both the north and north east by a number of Germanic tribes as well as a newly emerging threat in the east, that of the Sassanid Persian Empire. The main sources we have for this period are the *Scriptores Historiae Augustae* (SHA) and the *New History* of Zosimus. The SHA, supposedly written by six authors but now believed to be the work of just a single person, is frustratingly full of half-truths and fantasy and one has to take much of what is said by the anonymous author with a degree of healthy scepticism. Zosimus was another sixth century Eastern Roman historian who relied on often conflicting accounts by other historians such as Olympiodorus, Dexippus and Eunapius in his history.

The Goths took advantage of the situation and they began to make extensive raids into the Empire, both by land and sea. Eleven years after the first incursion, Marcianople, an important City located in the province of Thracia (later under Diocletian it became the major city of the province of Moesia Secunda) was attacked by two Gothic kings, Guntheric and Argaith, who sacked it. Just a year later in AD 250, Cniva, another Gothic king, crossed the Danube at the location of the city of Oescus, moved south and sacked a number of cities, the chief amongst them being Philippopolis. Cniva over-wintered in the vicinity of Philippopolis and the next year he and his army encountered several Roman armies who had some initial success against Cniva and his Goths. Cniva's most notable achievement was when he encountered the Emperor Decius and his army at Abrittus and thoroughly routed it, killing Decius in the process.[2] It must be remarked here that we have for the first time a 'Barbarian' army that was not only able to spend the best part of a year on Roman soil without being ejected but was able to destroy a Roman army sent to defeat it, killing the Emperor leading it in the process, a chilling premonition of events to come 125 years later.

A few short years later, Gothic fleets, sailing from their anchorages on the northern shore of the Black Sea, attacked the Roman provinces of Cappadocia and Pontus et Bithynia on the southern coast of the same sea, these attacks happening sometime between AD 253 and 257. An initial attack on the coastal city of Pityus was unsuccessful, but a later attack on Pityus saw it ravaged along with the city of Trapezus. These early sea-borne raids were carried out by a tribe known as the 'Boranoi', who may or may not have been a Gothic tribe. Certainly by the third year of these sea raids the Goths themselves were joining in on such sea attacks, and they not only attacked the coastal towns and cities but penetrated deep into the provinces along the south coast of the Black Sea as well as the western coast of that sea, plundering the cities of Nicomedia, Nicaea, Apamea, Chalcedon and Prusa. Zosimus claimed that not only were the cities and towns on the southern coast of the Black Sea ravaged by the Goths during this period but that the Goths also forced the straits of the Bosporus and ravaged the coasts of the province of Asia, much of Greece and even attacked Italy itself. In the east the Goths even managed to plunder the suburbs of Antioch. Unfortunately this Gothic land and sea assault coincided with an invasion of the eastern part of the Roman Empire by the Sassanids led by their capable King of Kings Sharpur I. And if that were not enough, the Empire was being torn apart internally by a rapid succession of usurpers.[3]

From AD 259 the situation worsened; as Zosimus put it: '... the Scythians united, congregating from every nation and people into one body. Then one section of their forces ravaged Illyricum and sacked the cities there, whilst the other invaded Italy and marched as far as Rome.'[4] Amidst this upheaval the Emperor Valerian took the field against Sharpur I, king of Sassanid Persia. The Sassanids had thrown off the yoke of Parthian rule and ruled over a vast territory that extended from the Euphrates River in the west to the east of India. The Sassanids believed that they were the successors to the Achaemenid Persian Empire and laid claim to all of Roman territory in the East and even laid claim to Greece itself! Valerian was defeated and taken prisoner by Sharpur personally. Plagues swept through many cities of the Empire, reducing the population even further. The Empire was tottering and on the verge of collapse.

The western Emperor, Gallienus, was battling the barbarian tribes north of the Danube when Valerian was taken prisoner and, with the aid of citizens in the Italian cities who had taken up arms, he managed to drive the Goths out of Italy. By AD 267 when the situation looked utterly desperate, Gallienus took the offensive against the Goths, who by now had looted and pillaged their way through Greece, even capturing Athens by siege. Gallienus sent Odaenathus, King of Palmyra and ally of Rome, eastwards to deal with Sharpur's invasion, whilst Gallienus himself carried the war against the Goths in Italy. Unfortunately Odaenathus and Gallienus fell victims to plots and both were dead by AD 268, despite their successes.[5]

At this same time the Goths raised a huge army, a combined force of Goths, Heruli (another Gothic tribe) and Peuci (a Germanic tribe) numbering some 320,000 warriors. They embarked on 6,000 ships (according to Zosimus).[6] Even taking the usual ancient historians' inflated numbers into account this was possibly the largest Gothic invasion before AD 376. At this point fate now intervened in favour of the Romans. The Gothic fleet sailed across the Black Sea and the warriors they carried attacked the walled city of Tomi. Instead of the usual storming and plundering, the Goths were unexpectedly repulsed by the defenders. The Gothic horde then marched inland and attacked Marcianople, and yet again they were repulsed by the defending troops and citizens. The Goths took back to their ships where they attempted to sail through the straights of the Propontis. However, due to the combination of too swift a current and too many ships the crews became confused and collisions occurred between the vessels, leading to a large number of ships sinking with their crews and warrior contingents. Whilst the Goths

were reeling from these unexpected disasters Claudius II was proclaimed
Emperor. This able man took the war to the Goths and engaged them near
Naissus. Although the Romans took heavy losses at the Battle of Naissus
itself, they managed to kill many Goths afterwards in ambushes.[7] Claudius
was acclaimed as 'Gothicus' as a result of this victory but he did not live long
to savour it. Whilst the Romans were harrying the remaining Goths out of
Greece, plague swept through the Gothic and Roman ranks, killing many
including Claudius himself.[8]

Despite this setback fortune again smiled upon the Romans as yet another
able man was proclaimed Emperor, Aurelian. When he was acclaimed he
not only had to contend with the Goths and other Germanic tribes, but also
a major revolt in the East where Odaenathus' wife, Zenobia, had rebelled
after her husband's death. Aurelian dealt with both problems with ruthless
efficiency.[9] Unfortunately for the Roman Empire, this most able and martial
Emperor fell victim to a plot and was murdered shortly after celebrating his
triumph in Rome.[10]

Tacitus was then proclaimed Emperor in AD 276, just at the moment
when the Goths again overran Asia from Cilicia to the Black Sea. Tacitus
marched against them, defeating part of the Goths in battle and leaving his
General Florianus to deal with the rest.[11] Yet again, plots arose and Tacitus
was murdered as he was about to march back to Rome. Florianus' campaign
against the Goths was interrupted when he was proclaimed Emperor in
Rome. Civil war broke out as the East chose Probus as a rival Emperor.
Probus prevailed and Florianus became another in a long line of short
reigned Emperors. It is not clear whether Probus engaged the Goths or not,
he certainly engaged a number of barbarian tribes, including the Alamanni,
Franks, Burgundians, Bastarnae and Vandals.[12]

The Goths from the death of Probus to the accession of Constantine

Probus, like those before him, fell foul of a plot and was murdered in AD 282.
Carus was proclaimed Emperor by the Danubian legions of Raetia and
Noricum. Although nearly 60 years of age he was an active man and led
an army across the Danube against the Sarmatians and then launched a

full scale invasion of Sassanid Persia, capturing two of the most important Sassanid cities, Seleucia and the capital Ctesiphon. He does not appear to have faced the Goths, and the Goths are not mentioned during his short reign, for he died under curious circumstances in AD 283.[13] During Carus' reign a man by the name of Diocles rose to the rank of commander of the Protectores Domestici, the elite personal bodyguard cavalry of the Emperor. Diocles received a consulship from Carus in AD 283, further elevating his position. Carus' sons Carinus and Numerian became Western and Eastern Emperors respectively upon Carus' death. Numerian died under mysterious circumstances during the march back from Ctesiphon in AD 284 and Diocles was proclaimed Emperor by the troops, despite the fact that Carinus was still a legitimate Emperor. Diocles adopted the name Gaius Aurelius Valerius Diocletianus, better known as Diocletian. Diocletian and Carinus gathered their forces and in AD 285 both armies met at Margus, not far from modern Belgrade. Diocletian's army was badly mauled by that of Carinus and just when all seemed lost, news spread that Carinus was dead, struck down by one of his own officers. Carinus' army ceased fighting and swore allegiance to Diocletian. Diocletian was now the sole ruler of the Roman Empire.[14]

Diocletian set about making a number of radical changes not only to the organization and running of the Empire but also to the Roman army itself (see Chapter Fifteen). Having no son when he acceded to the purple, Diocletian played one of his master-strokes. He promoted a younger, more military minded senior officer to rank of Caesar and Filius Augusti. This was in AD 285 and that officer's name was Maximian. Maximian was further promoted to Augustus in April AD 286 when another internal crisis sprang up in the form of one Carausius, one of Maximian's generals whose troops under his command had declared him as Augustus.[15]

The Goths had been largely quiet from the reign of Probus but we hear of them again during the five years Maximian was campaigning in the West as one of the tribes he fought against were the Heruli. Whilst Maximian was away in the West, Diocletian began a series of campaigns in the East. The Sarmatians had been under increasing pressure from the Goths and other tribes north of the Danube and they were being forced south, leading to incursions across the Danube itself. Diocletian fought at least two campaigns against the Sarmatians between AD 285 and 289.[16] It was during this period

Diocletian began fortifying the Rhine, Danube and Eastern frontiers with new forts and refortifying strategic cities. It was also probably around about this time that changes to the Roman army were begun, changes that Constantine would continue and complete (see Chapter Fifteen). Diocletian also raised two new Legions, the Herculanii and Iovanii, and began the reformation of the Praetorian Guards, replacing them with new units.[17]

And in yet another master stroke, on 1 March AD 293 Diocletian promoted one of his most experienced military officers, Gaius Galerius, to the title of Caesar at Sirmium, whilst at the same time Maximian promoted Marcus Favius Constantius to the title of Caesar at Milan. These new appointments were to act as loyal understudies to the Emperors, to ensure if anything happened to either Diocletian or Maximian then a smooth transition would occur and hopefully prevent the problems that had plagued the Empire during the reigns of the preceding Emperors.

The Goths again began to make their presence felt during this period as Diocletian campaigned against several Gothic tribes, the Taifali and the Tervingi, from AD 289 to 291.[18] It is during this period that Kulikowski believes the Tervingi rise to power began. He linked the campaigns against the Sarmatians and the Carpi as evidence of those tribes being displaced from their homelands by the more powerful Tervingi Goths. This is not an unrealistic view; exactly this happened to the Alans and the Greuthungi and Tervingi Goths when the Huns began to drive them out of their lands during the late AD '360s'. Kulikowski's view that the Romans may have had a hand in the Tervingi's rise to power may also be correct when we look at Valens' own meddling in Gothic affairs in Chapters Four and Five. The last campaign of AD 291 saw a period of relative peace with few, if any, Gothic incursions. It may well be the Goths had their hands full north of the Danube with the other tribes they were extending their influence over.

Another possible reason for the Goths remaining quiet was that they found peaceful employment with the Romans from the mid-AD '280s' as Jordanes claimed. According to Jordanes, the Goths provided support in a campaign against the Sassanids and Diocletian and Maximian may have had Gothic support when the Tetrarchy started to breakdown after they abdicated in AD 305. A period of civil war broke out as the newly appointed Emperors did not have the full support required to keep them on their respective thrones.

After the dust settled in AD 313 only two claimants remained standing, in the East the anti-Christian Licinius, and in the West the Christian sympathizer Constantine. Although relations between the two were initially neutral, the situation between them broke down and another civil war broke out. Both had support from barbarians, Franks served in Constantine's army, whilst Goths served with Licinius. By AD 324 there was only one sole ruler of the Roman Empire, Constantine, known to history as Constantine the Great.[19]

The Goths from Constantine to the reign of Valens

Constantine continued the reformation of both the Empire and its army, making sweeping changes in both areas (see Chapter Fifteen). Two years before becoming sole Emperor, Constantine crossed the Danube to deal with the Sarmatians, killing their King Rausimodus, and capturing those who were not slain during the battle.[20] This led to further campaigns against the Goths and Sassanids after AD 324, despite the claims of Zosimus to the contrary.[21] Constantine inflicted a massive defeat on the Goths in AD 332 and imposed a treaty upon them that included a condition that the Goths were to provide troops upon request.[22] Jordanes' claim that the Goths supplied manpower to assist in building the new capital of Constantinople due to this treaty may not be as fanciful as his similar claim that they '…furnished him forty thousand men to aid him against various peoples. This body of men, namely, the Allies, and the service they rendered in war are still spoken of in the land to this day.'[23] There is no doubt that the defeat inflicted upon the Goths was such that they did not trouble the Romans for at least the next thirty years (however see below). This did not prevent the Goths under their King Geberich from further extending their territory into the land of the Asdingi Vandals where the Goths inflicted a crushing defeat upon them. This caused the remnants of that tribe to petition Constantine who settled them in Pannonia.[24] Gothic expansion continued under King Hermanaric, who had succeeded to the throne of the Amali upon the death of Geberich. Jordanes claimed that Hermanaric conquered the following tribes – the Gothescytha; Thiudos; Inaunxis; Vasinabroncae; Merens; Mordens; Imniscaris; Rogas; Tadzans; Athaul; Navego; Bubegenae; Coldae; Venethi; Aesti and the Heruli, extending Gothic rule from the Black Sea to the Baltic.[25]

By 337 Constantine was making preparations for an invasion of Sassanid Persia. Whilst there is no direct evidence that Constantine had approached the Goths for support, it would seem highly probable that the treaty obligations placed upon them would have led to them supplying manpower for the invasion. Constantine had advanced to Nicomedia where he fell ill and died on 22 May AD 337. There is some confusion over whether the campaign had got underway before he died in 337 but his death put the campaign on hold. Constantine's sons, Constantius, Constantine and Constans, divided the Empire between them but they soon fell out and war again wracked the Empire. Constantine fell in battle against Constans in AD 340 whilst Constans was murdered in a coup in AD 350, leaving Constantius to face Magnentius who had usurped Constans. Constantius emerged the victor in AD 353 after one of the bloodiest civil war battles in Roman history, a battle that was to have far reaching consequences for the Roman state as it would take many years for the Empire to bring its army back up to strength. The conflict between Magnentius and Constantius left Gaul overrun by barbarian tribes who took full advantage of the chaos in that province (there is the suspicion that Constantius did nothing to prevent this as a punishment for that province's support for Magnentius). Like his father before him Constantius now became sole ruler of the Roman Empire after Magnentius' death in AD 353.

Before the death of his father, Constantius had been sent during the AD '330s' by Constantine to engage the Goths across the Danube and he was so successful that he not only caused the displacement of a reputed 100,000 Goths but he also received hostages including Ariaric, one of the Gothic kings' sons.[26] This led to a period of peace between Rome and the Goths that went almost undisturbed for the next thirty-five years. Although there is no mention of Constantius engaging in any further campaigns against the Goths, he did campaign successfully over the Danube against the Sarmatians and the Limogantes, removing them both as future threats against the Empire. Constantius may have enlisted Gothic support in these campaigns from both the Taifali and the Heruli. Ammianus records an approach Constantius made to the Taifali, Ammianus also further recorded that there were auxiliary units called the Taifali and Heruli in the Roman army at that time.[27]

Constantius had raised his nephew Gallus to the rank of Caesar in the East whilst dealing with the issues in the West. Gallus proved a political disaster and Constantius had Gallus murdered in AD 355. Problems again arose in the east when Sharpur II, King of Kings of the Sassanid Empire, who had proved troublesome during Constantine's reign, went on the offensive. At the same time the Allemanni, a Germanic tribe living north of the Rhine, ravaged Gaul and occupied a number of towns and cities. Constantius realized he could not fight on two fronts and so in AD 356 he promoted his scholarly nephew Julian to the rank of Caesar and tasked Julian with dealing with the situation in Gaul. This may have been a cynical act on Constantius' behalf as Julian had no military experience, he was more attuned to the world of books and arts and therefore was likely to suffer a 'mishap' against the barbarians he was to engage, without Constantius having to resort to other means to remove him.[28] Unfortunately for Constantius, and fortunately for the West at that time, Julian proved to be a charismatic leader of men and from AD 357 he successfully engaged the Alamanni in a number of battles, the most notable being Argentoratum, smashing that tribe and capturing many nobles and kings. He also engaged other tribes north of the Rhine, including the Quadi, Salli and Franks, successfully dealing with them also. Julian restored not only the Rhine frontier but also brought Gaul back under Roman control, much to the delight of its inhabitants and to the chagrin of Constantius. The situation could not last long between them and when in February AD 360 Constantius sent a demand to Julian for a large number of Western troops for a proposed offensive against the Sassanids, the troops under Julian's command rebelled and compelled Julian to become a reluctant usurper.[29]

Julian and Constantius both gathered their forces and marched towards each other but fortune smiled upon Julian again as Constantius fell ill on the march and died after reaching Mopsuestia in Cilicia on 3 November AD 361. On his deathbed Constantius named Julian as his heir, which probably surprised many at the time, no doubt also surprising Julian. Constantius wished for the Empire he had defended from all manner of foreign invaders for so long not to have to undergo the upheaval of another round of civil war and at least under Julian, who against the odds had proved both militarily and politically successful in the West, the Empire may well remain safe and secure.

Julian, once sole Emperor, embarked on two crusades, the reintroduction of Pagan worship, and the destruction of the Sassanids and their King of Kings, Sharpur II. In both of these enterprises he was spectacularly unsuccessful. Christianity had become the major religion of the Roman Empire from the time of Constantine and Constantius was a fervent worshiper of that faith and called many synods, much to the disgust of those with Pagan leanings such as Libanius; even Ammianus expressed some qualms about this in his description of Constantius after his death.[30] Constantius had been rather too successful in this enterprise and Julian found a great deal of resistance to his efforts at reintroducing the old religions. He also began to raise an army to finally deal with Sharpur, possibly with the intent of placing Sharpur's brother Hormisdas on the throne as one who would be a friend to Rome. He was ready to launch the offensive in AD 363 and marched with his army, possibly at least 60,000 strong over the Euphrates.[31] Ironically this army included those same troops who had refused to come to Constantius when he had ordered them to three years before. Julian appears to have used his family connection to Constantius, and hence to Constantine, to request troops from the Goths as he had a contingent of 'Skythian Auxilliaries' or 'Goths' with him.[32] Although the campaign met with a number of early successes, the closer to Ctesiphon he marched the stronger the Sassanid resistance became and he had not managed to face Sharpur in battle. Sharpur was in fact hastening towards Ctesiphon with a large army; Julian appears to have lost his nerve at this point and after an unsuccessful attempt to capture Ctesiphon he began to march his army back towards Roman territory. He never made it, he was mortally wounded in a major skirmish at Maranga against Sassanid forces that were harrying the rear of his column and he died from his wounds on 26 June AD 363, just a few short months into the campaign. What became of the 'Scythians' under Julian's command is not recorded, presumably they made their own way back to their homelands or remained in the Empire and were enrolled into the ranks of the army.[33]

On 27 June AD 363 the army promoted one of the senior officers, Jovian, to the rank of Augustus. This was due to Julian having no heir, although it was claimed at the time that Julian had in fact named a relative, Procopius, as his heir. Jovian was faced with the awful task of trying to get a large Roman army back to safe territory intact. The only way he could do this was to enter into a humiliating peace treaty with Sharpur that ceded territory back to the Sassanids, territory that Constantius had fought so hard to protect. Along with the territory went cities such as Singara and Nisibis, where so much Roman and Sassanid blood had been spilt. Constantius must have been spinning in his tomb!

Jovian's reign was short, he was dead by 17 February AD 364 and, leaving no heir, again the army took it upon themselves to raise one of their number to the purple. The first candidate refused, citing ill health and advanced age, the next candidate was Valentinian, a capable man of proven military prowess. And so on 26 February AD 364 Valentinian was proclaimed Emperor of the Roman Empire. Had Valentinian thought he was going to be sole Imperator he was badly mistaken. The army, not wishing to be left in the situation they faced when both Julian and Jovian died, demanded he take someone to be co-Emperor. And so, on 28 March 364 his younger brother Valens was raised to the purple. The Empire was divided between them, Valentinian taking the Western half of the Empire whilst Valens reigned over the East.[34]

Remarkably, the barbarian tribes beyond the Rhine and Danube had taken very little advantage of the situation from the death of Julian to the elevation of Valentinian and Valens. Such were memories of the defeats inflicted upon them by Constantius and Julian whilst they were still alive, and the forces left behind to defend the frontiers, that the Barbarians dared not act against the Romans.

This situation would not last long.

Chapter Three

Valens, Procopius, and the Goths

As discussed in Chapter Two, Valentinian proclaimed Valens as Augustus on 28 March AD 364 in the suburb of Constantinople known as Hebdomum, or Septimum due to its distance from the city itself. No sooner than Valens had donned the purple than both he and Valentinian were struck down with fevers, the cause of which was unknown but there was a suspicion that it was due to sorcery. However, a thorough investigation instigated by the two Emperors found no evidence of this.[1] They spent the winter of 364 'in perfect harmony'. Valentinian then divided the Empire and its generals between both Emperors; Valentinian gave himself the Western half of the Empire that included the provinces of Gaul, Africa, Britain, Greece and Italy, with Valens being given the rest of the provinces in the East. When these arrangements had been concluded Valentinian made his way to Mediolanum in Gaul, whilst Valens established his court in Constantinople.[2]

If Valens thought he was now going lead a life of ease and luxury he was very much mistaken. For, as Ammianus put it 'At this time, as if trumpets were sounding the war-note throughout the whole Roman world, the most savage peoples roused themselves and poured across the nearest frontiers. At the same time the Alamanni were devastating Gaul and Raetia, the Sarmatae and Quadi Pannonia, while the Picts, Saxons, Scots and Attacotti were harassing the Britons with constant disasters. The Austoriani and other Moorish tribes raided Africa more fiercely than ever and predatory bands of Goths were plundering Thrace and Pannonia. The King of the Persians was laying hands on Armenia, hastening with mighty efforts to bring that country again under his sway.'[3] Of course Ammianus was using hindsight when referring to events throughout the reigns of both Valens and Valentinian until their deaths, but even so it sounded suspiciously as if the Crisis of the Third Century was about to be repeated in the fourth!

No sooner had both Emperors taken up their residences than serious problems arose. The Alamanni, a Germanic tribe living north of the Rhine, who had been quiet since their defeat at the hands of Julian, became hostile and bands of them crossed over the Rhine frontier. The cause of this incursion was due to the Alamanni being given tributes that were inferior to that which they had been accustomed to receiving. And to add even more insult to the injury, the Alamannic envoys sent to receive the gifts were badly treated by Ursatius, a *Magister Officiorum* (Master of the Court) of Valentinian's court. Said envoys on returning to their homes exaggerated the insults and this roused the Alamanni to seek revenge.[4]

At approximately the same time, Procopius, who I mentioned in Chapter Two as being named by Julian as his heir, 'started a revolution' and made a play for Valens' throne. Valentinian received this news on 1 November AD 364. Valentinian sent Dagalaifus, an officer promoted by Jovian to the rank of *Magister Armorum* (Master of Arms), with an army to deal with the Alamanni threat, whilst Valentinian himself pondered on what to do about Procopius. There appeared to be some confusion as to the circumstances surrounding Procopius' bid for power. Valentinian was unsure whether Valens had been killed and that was the catalyst for Procopius to declare himself, as the only report he received was from Aequitius, a *Comes* (Count, a senior officer) (later to become a *Magister*, a senior general) who himself had heard it in a report from an Antonius, a tribune commanding troops in Dacia who had himself only heard vague accounts from another, unnamed source.

Valentinian initially made preparations to head East to prevent Procopius advancing into Pannonia, the province that was Valentinian and Valens' birthplace. However, he was persuaded to head back to Gaul to deal with the Alamanni threat, leaving Valens, if he were still alive, to deal with Procopius by himself.[5]

Procopius was a cousin of Julian's, on Julian's mother's side. He could claim some legitimacy for both the thrones of Valentinian and Valens as Julian had been sole Emperor upon his death. There were even rumours that Julian had ordered Procopius to assume power should things go badly for the Romans during the invasion of Sassanid Persia.[6] Upon learning of Julian's death, and the army having declared Jovian as Emperor, Procopius, fearing he would be put to death as a potential rival, fled and sought refuge with friends in Chalcedon. From here he was able to gather information about Valens and the state of the Empire in secret.

Events in the East were taking a turn for the worse as Valens appeared to be burdening the citizens of the East, rich and poor alike, with heavy taxes. And, at a most opportune time for Procopius, the Goths, quiet beyond the Danube since the heavy defeat inflicted upon them during the reign of Constantine, were rumoured to be making preparations to invade Thrace and the territory around.[7] Valens, having already made preparations to head into Syria, was in Bithynia when he was informed about the Gothic plans and was forced to send troops to the areas where he believed the Goths would most likely be heading for. Procopius took advantage of the situation and made his play for power. He made contact with officers within two legions, the Divitenses and the Tungricani Iuniores and upon entering Constantinople he was acclaimed Emperor with their support.[8]

A number of 'Barbarian' tribes pledged their support to Procopius, citing his relationship to Constantius and Julian as the pretext for this. The only tribe that gets a specific mention are the Goths, whose kings sent either 3,000[9] or 10,000 troops to aid Procopius.[10] It appears that Procopius had entered into negotiations with the Goths who had a short time before crossed the Danube and were ravaging Thrace and Pannonia. Procopius used his relationship to the relatives of Constantine to force the Goths to adhere to the treaty agreement of AD 332 and to support his cause with troops. The troops they sent would have no doubt have been of great use to Procopius in his claim to the throne of the East, both in military and political terms.

Valens was about to leave Caesarea to go to his residence in Antioch when he was brought news of events in Constantinople. He was persuaded to go to Galatia to try and restore the situation whilst he still could. Procopius in the meantime had received embassies from all over the Empire, one such bearing the false news that Valentinian was dead and that the whole empire was his for the taking. Procopius' forces were increased when some infantry and cavalry units sent by Valens to deal with the Goths in Thrace, joined with the forces in Constantinople supporting Procopius. Procopius in the meantime had duped Julius, commander of the army in Thrace, into coming to Constantinople where he managed to convince Julius' men to desert and in one fell swoop Procopius gained the forces Julius had commanded. Not everything went Procopius' way however. He had sent men to bribe the commander and officers of the forces in Illyricum, but the overall commander, Aequitius, remained loyal to Valens. Aequitius' forces killed the men sent by Procopius and blockaded the passes leading into the Northern provinces.[11]

Valens, now in Galatia, descended into the depths of despair and considered stepping down as Emperor. Being persuaded against this action by those still loyal to him, he roused himself to action and sent the Jovii and Victores, both notable Palatine Auxilia units to attack Procopius and his men. These two units found Procopius, with the Divitenses Legion and some deserters at Mygdus by the banks of the Sangarius River. Both sides engaged each other before Procopius personally stood between both forces and gave such a speech that the Jovii and Victores units switched sides and joined the army of Procopius. Procopius then sent a turncoat Tribune called Rumitalca with a fleet to capture Helenopolis and this force then went on to capture Nicaea. Valens responded by sending Vadomarius, a former king of the Alamanni and now a general in Roman service, to recapture Nicaea, whilst Valens went to lay siege to Chalcedon. A sally from Nicaea, led by Rumitalca, burst through Vadomarius' besieging force and threatened the rear of Valens' own besieging army that was nearby. Valens, receiving reports of the approach of Rumitalca, retreated swiftly and made a rapid escape to the safety of Ancyra where he learnt that Lupicinus, *Magister Militum* of the Orient under Jovian, was approaching with reinforcements. Valens despatched Arintheus, the best general who was still loyal to him, to take charge of this new army and to lead it against the forces of Procopius. Arintheus marched against Procopius and whilst en route encountered a force of auxiliary units loyal to Procopius, possibly including the Jovii and Victores who had initially been loyal to Valens, but instead of attacking them, used his authority to persuade them to throw their leader in chains and come over to his side.[12]

The region of Bithynia now having fallen into Procopius' hands, led Procopius to send troops to capture the city of Cyzicus, where Venustus, a state treasury official, had taken refuge with the pay for the troops stationed in the Orient. Procopius' forces managed to storm the city once the protective chain across the entrance to the port had been broken. Procopius spent the winter in luxury in Cyzicus and this became his undoing for it allowed Valens to regroup his forces for an offensive in the spring of AD 366.[13]

The spring of AD 366 saw an invigorated Valens advance with his army into Galatia and thence on to Lycia where he planned to attack Procopius' forces led by Gomoarius that were now stationed there. Unfortunately for Valens, these forces had with them the daughter of Constantius II, born after his death, and also Constantius' wife Faustina. These 'trophies' spurred Procopius' troops to fight with stubborn determination; they were after all defending the relatives of a former Emperor who was much admired by those troops. At this point Valens had a stroke of genius. He persuaded the venerable General and ex-consul Arbitio, who had served under both Constantine and Constantius, to come out of retirement and this most respected man railed against Procopius and the troops under him. Arbitio's arguments against Procopius' rebellion persuaded Gomoarius to desert to the camp of Valens, using the excuse that he had been captured by some of Valens' men. Valens, now confident of victory, marched to Phrygia and attacked Procopius' army. At the height of the battle, at the critical point where victory could have gone to either side, Agilo, one of the commanders of Procopius' army, without warning, deserted to Valens' side. Most of Procopius' army followed suit and that was the end of Procopius' stab at the purple. He fled with a few followers into the night but the next morning these same companions bound him and took him to Valens' camp where he was immediately beheaded.[14]

There was to be no immediate cause for celebration as Marcellus, an officer of the Protectores Domesticii, the Emperors' guard unit, who was in charge of the garrison at Nicaea, made his own bid for the purple and captured Chalcedon. However, this new rebellion was short-lived as Aequitius marched swiftly to Philippopolis, where Marcellus had garrisoned troops, including the Goths that their kings had sent to support Procopius. Aequitius sent troops to capture Marcellus, which they had no trouble in doing. Marcellus was taken before Aequitius, scourged and then put to death, along with many of his companions. Thus ended the last serious threat to Valens' throne from within the Empire itself.[15]

It was telling that Procopius and Marcellus only aimed at Valens' throne, and not that of Valentinian's. Valens was considered by contemporary historians to be very much in his brother's shadow and, whilst not militarily incompetent, he was in no way as experienced in military matters as his brother Valentinian was. It was easier therefore for Procopius and Marcellus to take on Valens and strive for the throne of the East than attempt to take on the far more dangerous and able Valentinian.

Valens wreaked terrible retribution on those who had supported both Procopius and Marcellus, and very soon this retribution would extend to the Goths.

Chapter Four

Valens' Gothic Campaigns AD 367–369

T

he threat of the usurper Procopius having been removed, Valens turned his attention to other matters. To this end during AD 366 Valens despatched Victor, now *Magister Equitum* (Master of the Cavalry) beyond the Danube to the land of the Goths to enquire why they had broken their treaty with the Roman Empire by lending support to Procopius and attacking the armies of the legitimate Emperor. The Goths defended their actions by producing a letter written to them by Procopius stating he had assumed the role of Emperor of the East by virtue of his relationship to Constantine and thereby had elicited their support as per the treaty agreement. When Victor returned with this news Valens became incensed and set about raising an army to exact retribution upon them.[1]

By the spring of AD 367 all was ready and Valens moved with his army to the province of Moesia Secunda which was the one closest to the Danube bordering the Gothic lands. It was from here that Valens would launch his attack upon the traitorous Goths. On arriving in that province Valens pitched his camp at the fortress called Daphne on the banks of the Danube. A bridge was thrown over the Danube, it was constructed of boats lashed together on top of which was a planked surface over their decks. Using this Valens and his army crossed over totally unopposed. The reason for this soon became apparent, the Goths were fully aware of both his preparations for war and of his coming.[2] This was either due to Roman deserters fleeing to the Goths informing them of what they knew, or it could have been Gothic recruits in the Roman army returning home on leave informing their fellow tribesmen of what was about to happen. This was unfortunately a fairly common occurrence (see Chapter Eight). Valens, now on the northern side of the Danube, found no armies to vanquish, the Goths having taken themselves to the safety of the mountains. There was precious little Valens could do apart from despatching Arintheus, now promoted to *Magister Peditum* (Master of the Infantry) with some detachments to scour the land for any straggling Gothic families that could be used as potential hostages. Valens returned back over the Danube during the summer without having achieved anything of note.

The following year Valens yet again attempted to invade the territory of the Goths. He had moved further East along the Danube and Ammianus had him 'near a village of the Carpi in a permanent camp which he had made'.[3] The campaign came to an abrupt end due to the Danube flooding and he was forced to break camp and make his way to Marcianople where he spent the winter of AD 368.[4]

One cannot fault Valens' persistence and determination to deal with the Goths, because he embarked on yet a third campaign against them in AD 369. This time he had positioned himself much further East, at the town on Novidunum on the banks of the Danube bordering the territory of the Greuthungi Goths. Valens and his army again crossed on a bridge of boats, and on this campaign Valens was much more successful. He engaged Athanaricus, an 'Iudex' or King of the Goths.[5] Athanaricus gathered an army and met Valens in battle. Valens inflicted a decisive defeat upon Athanaricus, who was forced to flee for his life.[6]

Valens, consulting with his advisors, sent envoys in the form of Victor, Commander of the Cavalry and Arintheus, Commander of the Infantry, to negotiate the terms of ending the war. They returned and informed Valens that Athanaricus had agreed to the terms that Valens had proposed and that a new peace treaty was to be entered into between the Goths and the Roman Empire. However, Athanaricus refused to cross the Danube to formally sign it, stating his father had forbidden him to cross the Danube and enter Roman territory under oath. And so it was arranged that both Valens and Athanaricus would meet in the centre of the Danube on boats where the treaty would be agreed and hostages exchanged. Whilst the spin given on this by Ammianus and Themistius was that it was a glorious victory and humbling of the Goths, one cannot help but notice that it was really Athanaricus who determined exactly where the treaty was to be concluded and that Valens had no option but to comply.[7]

The terms of this peace treaty had the tributes and gifts paid to the Goths since the treaty of AD 332 stopped, and trade between the Goths and Romans to only be carried out at two designated points on the Danube.[8] Valens also would begin the construction of defences along the Danube to prevent any further Gothic incursions. Whilst this at face value appears harsh, after all the loss of the yearly funds from the Romans must have hurt, the reality was that an integral part of the peace treaty imposed upon the Goths in 332 was removed, and this removal harmed the Romans far more. The new treaty did not place a condition upon the Goths to supply manpower to the Romans as and when needed. Whilst this clause ensured it would be impossible for any future usurper to contact the Goths and use any relationship to Constantine or his family as leverage to provide troops, it also would mean that any approach from Valens or any future Emperor would have to include inducements to do so.

What were Valens' aims and intentions for his Gothic campaigns? It is far too simplistic to suggest all that he wanted to do was to exact punishment upon them for the support they gave to Procopius. If this were the case then he would surely have not put so much time and effort into undertaking not one but three campaigns against them in so many years. The more reasonable suggestion would be that Valens wanted to inflict a crushing defeat upon the Goths with the intention of then exhorting them to abide by the treaty agreement of AD 332 and provide him with recruits for his Sassanid invasion force. It is patently clear that remaining north of the Danube on a permanent basis was not a part of Valens' campaign strategy; the fact that he returned back across the Danube each time he crossed it is proof of that. Of course there is always the case that Valens' campaigns were actually instigated not solely by the Goths' support of Procopius, but in fact were more to do with destabilizing the Goths to ensure that troublesome race did not take advantage of his moving troops East for his proposed invasion of Sassanid Persia. Even if this was not Valens' aim his campaigns against the Goths had the effect of weakening Athanaricus' rule over them and the defeat Athanaricus had suffered would cause problems for that Gothic ruler. An unintended side-effect of the conflict was that the defeat that was inflicted upon the Goths would have weakened their ability to put up a successful resistance against the Huns. In effect Valens' campaigns against the Goths did far more harm than good.

A far more reaching side-effect of the conclusion of the war was that sometime between the end of the conflict and the events of AD 376 a revolt appears to have taken place within the ranks of the Goths. A new contender for the King of the Tervingi Goths arose, one who was to become Valens' nemesis – Fritigern.

Chapter Five

Crisis Beyond the Danube AD 369–376

Whilst very little survives in the histories as to what happened beyond the Danube after the treaty of AD 369, and what does survive is confusing to say the least, there are some very clear indications that things took a turn for the worst for Athanaricus. Socrates Scholasticus wrote that the Tervingi Goths fell into a 'civil war' and split into two parts, one under the command of Athanaricus, the other under Fritigern.[1] It can be speculated that Athanaricus fell out of favour with at least a portion of the Goths following his defeat at the hands of Valens. The portion of the Goths that were disaffected with Athanaricus' rule were led by Fritigern, who was another Gothic chieftain. Fritigern took advantage of the unfavourable circumstances in which Athanaricus now found himself. He realized that the time was ripe to challenge Athanaricus, and made a play for the leadership of the Tervingi Goths. However, things did not go to plan as it appears that, much against his expectations, it was initially Fritigern who faced defeat at the hands of Athanaricus. This set-back led Fritigern to take the radical and unusual approach of making contact with Valens with a view to the Romans supporting him against Athanaricus.[2] One could see the appeal of this approach from Valens' side. It would remove Athanaricus as a future threat, and also put someone in charge of the Goths who owed Valens a huge debt in the process. Accordingly Valens despatched the army of Thrace beyond the Danube and with their support Fritigern achieved total victory over Athanaricus, forcing the now usurped former leader to flee with a small band of followers. In gratitude for Valens' support Fritigern converted to Christianity and persuaded those he led to convert as well.[3] The problem with this account, as given by Socrates, is that both Sozomen and Ammianus appear to place this rebellion to the time when Valens had granted leave for the Goths to cross the Danube and settle in Thrace, and in the case of Zosimus, after Valens had been defeated by Fritigern at Adrianople. My view is that the revolt by Fritigern must have taken place before AD 376. The reason for this being that it was Fritigern who arrived with the initial wave of Goths who appeared on the banks of the Danube. Athanaricus arrived with his Gothic contingent some time later at the banks of the same river and he was then initially refused permission to cross according to Ammianus. Athanaricus did not actually cross the Danube until much later, after the death of Valens had removed the potential threat to his life. This is a clear indication that by the time the Tervingi Goths arrived at the Danube in AD 376 they had split into two groups, who were at least allied towards each other.

The assistance Valens provided to Fritigern, and then the conversion of Fritigern and the Goths under his command to Valens' brand of Christianity, Arianism, I believe led to Valens viewing Fritigern in a particularly favourable light. I also believe that the esteem Valens held Fritigern in contributed to how Valens interacted with Fritigern from 376 onwards, and in turn directly affected how Valens acted towards the Goths themselves, especially on the eve of the Battle of Adrianople, of which I will discuss more in the relevant chapters.

Another evil to beset Athanaricus and the other Gothic chieftains north of the Danube was the troubling appearance of a new enemy, and one that was to cause them to leave their homelands for the perceived safety of what was the territory of the Roman Empire, which was technically another of their enemies.

The Goths who lived much further East, near the Caspian Sea, had for some time been engaged in low scale warfare against the steppe tribes that lived there, in the main the tribe known as the Halani or Alans. This warfare began to intensify as the Alans increasingly encroached on the Gothic sphere of influence. When this began is not entirely clear, but it could possibly as far back as the AD '350s' when pressure on the Sassanid north eastern frontier led to Sharpur II moving forces to counter a threat coming from that direction. This threat, nomadic tribes moving under external pressure, appears to have been caused by the same threat that had pushed the Alans out of their traditional homelands into the territory claimed by the Goths. And this threat had a name, the Huns.

Where the Huns came from, and who they were originally known as, is a hotly debated topic. Some of the earliest claims for the origin of the Huns are that they were in fact the Hsiung-nu, a tribe that lived on the vast Eurasian Steppe and that were attacked by another nomadic tribe, the Hsien-Pi, on instigation of the Chinese around AD 93. The Hsien-Pi absorbed many of them, forcing the rest who refused to join them to flee westwards. Other tribes are also mooted as the originators of Huns.[4]

It is not my place here to enter into this debate other than to say the matter is unlikely to be resolved unless by chance, typically via a lucky piece of archaeology. What I think we can do is to discount the Gothic version of the origin of the Huns as given by Jordanes – 'We learn from old traditions that their origin was as follows: Filimer, king of the Goths, son of Gadaric the Great, who was the fifth in succession to hold the rule of the Gatae after their departure from the island of Scandza, and who, as we have said, entered the land of Scythia with his tribe, found among his people certain witches, whom he called in his native tongue Haliurunnae. Suspecting these women, he expelled them from the midst of his race and compelled them to wander in solitary exile afar from his army. There the unclean spirits, who beheld them as they wandered through the wilderness, bestowed their embraces upon them, and begat this savage race, which dwelt at first in the swamps, a stunted, foul and puny tribe, scarcely human, and having no language save one which bore slight resemblance to human speech, such was the descent of the Huns who came to the country of the Goths.'[5]

Having the Huns born of witches after they had intercourse with demons would of course have had a certain appeal to Christian sentiments during that age!

Ammianus, who may never have actually seen a living Hun, wrote that the Huns lived 'beyond the Maeotic Sea near the ice-bound ocean'. He further noted that they were 'little known from ancient records'. He gives a most unflattering description of the Huns, full of the usual Roman prejudices – 'Since the cheeks of the children are deeply furrowed with the steel from their very birth, in order that the growth of hair, when it appears at the proper time, may be checked by the wrinkled scars, they grow old without beards and without any beauty, like eunuchs. They all have compact, strong limbs and thick necks, and are so monstrously ugly and misshapen, that one might take them for two-legged beasts or for the stumps, rough-hewn into images that are used into putting sides to bridges.'[6] A more derogatory description of a people it is hard to imagine! There are parallels with the description of Jordanes' Huns, and one has to consider if both historians had access to the same ancient texts when writing their histories, or indeed if Jordanes had a copy of Ammianus to hand when he compiled his history.

Of course, as with all history that has a basis in oral tradition, there may be more than a grain of truth mixed in amongst all the myth. Stunted growth and strange appearance may well be due to the diet of the Hunnic peoples, the conditions they were stated as living in and at least some of them practicing rituals that appears to have involved causing their children's heads to become elongated.[7]

Whatever the origins and appearance of the Huns, their impact upon the Goths and their neighbours cannot be denied or underestimated. The Huns overran the Alans and many joined their Hunnic conquerors in raiding the territory of the Greuthungi Goths. Other Alans appear to have fled to the side of their Gothic neighbours to aid in the Gothic attempts to repel the Hun invaders. Despite valiant efforts by Ermanaric (called Ermanarichus by Ammianus), a Gothic king who Jordanes stated was the one who conquered many other tribes during the Gothic rise to power, and was a redoubtable warrior and leader, the Goths were unable to stem the Hunnic tide. Ermanaric fell victim to treachery and was assassinated by the brothers of a woman from a different Gothic tribe whom he had ordered bound to two horses and torn in half.[8] After Ermanaric's death Vithimiris became the new Gothic King. He carried on the fight against the onslaught, this time his battles were against the Alans who were allied with the Huns, and of all peoples he had support from Hunnic mercenaries! Vithimiris fared no better than his predecessor and after a number of reverses he too fell in battle.[9] It's at this point in the histories that we now hear for the first time the names of Alatheus and Saphrax, who Ammianus noted were 'experienced generals known for their courage'. These two took charge of Vithimiris' son, Viderichus, who was at that time a small boy and in no way able to lead the Goths, and with their new charge these two generals retreated westwards.[10]

Athanaricus reappears at this point as 'the Chief of the Theruingi (Tervingi)'. He appears to have been in contact with the Greuthungi Goths, who, as I've previously noted in Chapter Three, Ammianus had stated

Athanaricus had at one time been one of their chieftains. Athanaricus contacted the Greuthungi and entered into an agreement with that tribe for a joint operation against the Huns. To this end it was agreed that both Gothic tribes would meet up and pitch their camps on the banks of the Danastius river, on the opposite side of which the Huns were operating. When this had been completed Athanarichus sent out a scouting party composed of 'men of high rank' who were to travel twenty miles and observe and report on the progress of the advancing Huns, whilst Athanarichus and the other Goths prepared for the impending battle. Unfortunately for the Goths the Huns were aware of the advance party and avoided them. The Huns moving at night, crossed the Danastius using a ford and totally surprised Athanarichus and his army, and utterly defeated them. Athanarichus survived the encounter and was forced to flee with the remnants of his army and they fled to the perceived safety of the nearby Carpathian Mountains.[11]

Once safely in the mountains Athanarichus attempted something novel to thwart the Huns. He either attempted to build field defences or repair some long deserted Roman fortifications. He would then use these as a defence against the Huns. Ammianus wrote that 'Athanarichus, troubled by this unexpected attack and still more through fear of what might come, had walls built high, skirting the lands of the Taifali from the banks of the river Gerasus as far as the Danube, thinking that by this hastily but diligently constructed barrier his security and safety would be assured.'[12] Heather believes that Athanarichus was actually attempting to repair the old Roman walls in the former province of Dacia known as the Limes Transalutanus.[13] This is not an unreasonable assumption, and if true it showed that the Goths were able to at least attempt to rebuild fortifications in the Roman style, if not build them from scratch. This audacious attempt by Athanaricus was in vain as he was assailed by constant Hunnic attacks. Athanarichus and his army were only saved from utter destruction by the fact that the Huns were so laden down by plunder that they were unable to catch the Goths fleeing from the unfinished fortifications.[14]

This was too much for the Goths under Athanarichus' command; he had once again failed to defeat the Huns and protect them from their enemy. The majority of them deserted and looked to others for leadership and protection. They choose another chieftain called Alavivus to lead them.

The Goths then held a deliberation and came to a conclusion. They would seek a new homeland, one that was unknown to the Huns and one that would provide a safe haven from Hunnic attacks. And the homeland they chose? The province of Thrace, south of the Danube, within the safety and protection of the Roman Empire, their former enemy![15]

Chapter Six

AD 367–376 – Friends and Enemies

I n the last chapter we were left with the Goths forced to make a radical choice about how to ensure their survival in the face of the onslaughting Huns. The decision they reached was one that was to have far-reaching implications not only for the Goths, but also for their former enemies the Romans.

However, before we go further we need to explore what was happening south of the Danube, within the borders of the Roman Empire itself from when Valens was embarked on his campaigns against the Goths from AD 367 until AD 376 when the Goths made their appeal to Valens to cross over into Thrace. These events were to have an on–going effect both on Valens' first Gothic campaigns and then what occurred afterwards. One event in particular would have a profound, if not fatal, influence on events from AD 376 onwards, that being the death of Valentinian. We cannot view in isolation the events that were discussed in the previous chapter without discussing what else was happening at the time as many of the events that were occurring within the Empire would have far reaching consequences once their impact was known by the time the Goths appeared on the banks of the Danube in AD 376.

During AD 367 large parts of Britain were overrun by a collection of tribes who lived not only beyond Hadrian's wall, but also across the Irish and North Seas and the English Channel. Those tribes were the Attacotti, Scotti, Picts and Saxons. These tribes ravaged Britain and in the process managed to kill both the Count of the Saxon Shore and the Duke of Britain, two of the highest ranking officials stationed there.[1] The Saxons and Franks, another Germanic tribe, also at this time raided the north west coast of Gaul facing Britain. Valentinian, Emperor of the West, was about to embark on a campaign against a Germanic tribe, the Alamanni, whose homelands were north of the Rhine when he heard the news and he ordered Severus, who was at that time the *Comes Domesticorum* (Count of the Household Troops), to undertake action to quell the rebellion in Britain.[2] However, Valentinian recalled Severus before he could undertake the campaign, probably so he could join Valentinian on his campaign against the Alamanni, and Jovinus, *Magister Equitum* (Master of the Horse) was appointed in Severus' place. Jovinus took so long to get the campaign to restore order to Britain underway that he was replaced by Theodosius, the father of the future Emperor Theodosius the Great.[3] Theodosius crossed the English Channel with a mixed force of legions and other troops and landed at the powerful fortress of Rutupiae (Richborough) in the extreme eastern tip of Kent, England. He waited there until four crack Auxilia Palatina units arrived, the Batavi, Heruli, Jovii and Victores.[4] Theodosius marched on to Londinium (London) which had been plundered by various bands of raiders who were still in the vicinity. Theodosius' troops completely routed all those they encountered, as the raiders were laden down with plunder. Such was the scale of his victory he was greeted by ecstatic crowds when he entered Londinium, where he set up his headquarters. From here he sent out proclamations throughout Britain, offering to pardon those troops who had either deserted or not bothered to return from leave when the barbarian bands invaded. Enough troops responded to this proclamation that Theodosius was able to both restore order and garrison the towns and cities of Britain once again.[5]

Also at this time the actions of Romanus, Governor of Africa led to an increase in raids by the nomadic tribes in that province and news of these problems was being deliberately withheld by Remigius, who was at that time *Magister Officiorum* (Marshal of the Court) and friend to Romanus. A notorious band of marauding brigands known as the Austoriani plundered various towns in Africa without interruption from Romanus and the armies under his command.[6] In Syria the Maratocupeni, who used audacious disguises to conceal their true intentions, plundered a number of towns and estates before being hunted down and totally wiped out along with their families.[7]

Isaurian brigands, relatively quiet since being severely dealt with during the reign of Constantius II,[8] erupted from their strongholds and ravaged Isauria and nearby regions. Musonius, *Asiae Vicarious* (Deputy Governor of Asia), raised a force of Diogmiae, or lightly equipped troops and attempted to deal with the raiders.[9] Unfortunately he was lured into an ambush and was killed. This was the trigger for action to finally be taken against the brigands who were forced back to their mountain strongholds where, after a truce was called for and terms and hostages exchanged they 'remained quiet for a long time, without venturing on any hostile act'.[10]

In AD 368 Rando, a prince of the Alamanni tribe, leading a small band of warriors, broke into the city of Mogontiacus (modern Mainz) whilst the Christians there were holding a ceremony. Many were captured by Rando and his men and taken away.[11] Valentinian responded to this audacious act by having the Alamanni King Vithicabius assassinated by one of that king's attendants who had been bribed to carry out the act.[12] This led to a decrease in raids by the Alamanni and gave Valentinian time to gather his forces for a campaign against them. Valentinian personally led the army that annihilated the Alamanni at Solicinium, but was almost killed in that battle.[13] After Solicinium armies led by his senior generals inflicted several other crushing defeats upon the Alamanni, killing one of their kings and forcing a treaty on them in the process. This quelled further incursions by that tribe and allowed Valentinian to put in place a plan to build a series of fortifications, the 'mile-forts', along the length of the Rhine westwards from the province of Raetia to the mouth of the Rhine where this entered the North Sea. And for the first time since the death of Julian, some of these fortifications were built on the north side of the Rhine itself, inside 'Barbarian' territory.[14]

Sharpur II, King of the Sassanid Persians, made an unexpected play for the Kingdom of Armenia during AD 368. He had tricked Arsaces, King of Armenia, to a banquet, captured him, and then had Arsaces murdered.[15] Sharpur placed Cylaces, a former Governor of Armenia, and Arrabannes, a former high-ranking military commander of that country, (who had both previously deserted to the Sassanids), in charge of Armenia. These two were charged with capturing Arsaces' wife and his son, Pap. Unfortunately for Sharpur, these duplicitous men secretly sided with the defenders of the fortified city of Artogerassa where Arsaces' wife and Pap were located and allowed the army sent to besiege the city to be destroyed by the defenders making a surprise night attack.[16] Pap was sent by his mother to Valens who initially kept him within the borders of the Empire but soon sent him back to rule Armenia 'without any emblems of royal rank'.[17] Sharpur invaded

Armenia with a large army and devastated that country. King Pap, in company of Cylaces and Arrabannes, fled and hid themselves in the remote countryside for five months. Sharpur, unable to capture Pap, resorted to laying siege to Artogerassa where Arsaces' wife and the royal treasury were located. Sharpur took the city by storm, capturing both Pap's mother and the treasury in the process, and then returned back to his own territory as winter was approaching.[18]

Valens despatched Count Arintheus with an army to the border of Armenia to render that country aid should Sharpur return on a second campaign the following year. Pap meanwhile, at the insistence of Sharpur, had both Cylaces and Arrabannes executed and sent their heads to Sharpur 'as a sign of his submission'.[19] Arintheus' forces prevented a second invasion of Armenia, and Sharpur sent envoys to Valens asking him not to interfere in the affairs of Armenia, in accordance with the arrangements of the treaty agreed by the Emperor Jovian.[20] Valens rejected this out of hand as Sharpur had clearly himself broken that very same treaty by invading Armenia.[21] Valens acted swiftly, sending Sauromaces, the former King of Hiberia who had been ousted by Sharpur, with Terentius, a high-ranking Roman general and twelve legions to Hiberia to reinstate Sauromaces to the throne of that country. Sharpur was naturally incensed by this course of events and began to raise an army with aid from nations who bordered his own.[22]

The situation in the East must have drawn away forces that Valens had planned to use against the Goths at the same time Sharpur had made his play for Armenia and this might go some way to explain the overall lack of a stunning success Valens had during his campaigns from AD 367 to AD 369 against the Goths.

In AD 370 the Saxons, after raiding Britain, then turned their attention on the northern coastal towns of Gaul.[23] The local forces under the command of Nannenus could not contain the Saxons, Nannenus, who was himself wounded in an encounter, sent a request to Valentinian for reinforcements. Valentinian despatched Severus, *Magister Peditum*, with enough troops for the task to aid Nannenus.[24] Severus' force so terrified the Saxons that they begged for peace and pleaded for negotiations to begin before any fighting took place. A truce was agreed and the Saxons were allowed to return to their homelands by an overland route.[25] However, Severus despatched part of the army to overtake the Saxons and ambush them. Unfortunately, the Romans hidden in ambush revealed their presence too soon and alerted the Saxons to their presence. The Saxons would have wiped them out had not a troop of Roman heavily armoured cavalry (*Catafractarii*), who were also sent to ambush the Saxons should they have taken another route, intervened and with their support the Roman infantry not only rallied but completely annihilated the Saxon horde.[26]

Valentinian however was not done with the Alamanni, and devised a plan that would have dealt with them and their troublesome King Macrianus had it worked. Valentinian sent envoys to the Burgundians, another Germanic tribe whose territory bordered that of the Alamanni north of the Rhine. The envoys carried letters from Valentinian to the Kings of the Burgundians asking them to attack the Alamanni, and if they did so Valentinian would cross the Rhine with an army so that both combined forces would crush the Alamanni once and for all. The Burgundians were only too keen to agree to this plan; they claimed a certain kinship with the Romans and had various unresolved disputes with the Alamanni.[27] For whatever reason, despite the Burgundians sticking faithfully to their side of the bargain, Valentinian failed to turn up at the appointed time and place where both sides were to meet before descending on the Alamanni. Despite sending envoys imploring Valentinian to at least provide them with a safe escort home, no Roman army appeared and the Burgundians returned home in furious indignation.[28] When the Burgundian kings learnt of this they killed all the Roman prisoners and hostages in their possession. Meanwhile the Romans took full advantage of the situation. Whilst the Burgundians were returning to their homelands their progress scattered the Alamanni who were in their way, allowing Theodosius, now *Magister Equitum*, to move through Raetia with an army and he slaughtered or captured all the Alamanni that were in his path.[29]

If this were not enough, there was dissent and rumblings in the 'Eternal City' of Rome itself. The cause of this was the machinations of Maximinus, whom Valentinian had promoted to Prefect of Rome, and his cohort in crime, Leo, who was later to be promoted to the rank of *Magistrum Officiorum*. These two men caused others to make wide ranging accusations against various nobles, soothsayers, senators and others stating that they were poisoners, adulterers, practitioners of sorcery etc. Many were tortured at a decree of Valentinian, others were executed whilst a lucky few were banished.[30] Women of noble birth were similarly accused of fornication and adultery and suffered grisly fates.[31] Simplicius of Hemona, who succeeded Maximinus, continued in a similar vein, causing noble women and men alike to suffer terribly. The crimes of Maximinus, Simplicius and all the others who caused fear and woe to descend upon the Eternal City finally had justice meted out to them in a like kind under the reign of Valentinian's son Gratian when he became Emperor.[32]

In AD 371 Sharpur again led his army into Roman territory, this time he invaded Mesopotamia with an army much larger than the one that he had invaded Armenia with in AD 368. Valens despatched Trajanus and Vadomarius, who had formerly been a King of the Alamanni, with an equally large force and both armies met at a place called Vagabanta where Sharpur and his army were defeated by the Romans.[33] A truce was called and Sharpur returned back with his army to winter at his capital of Ctesiphon.[34] Valens moved to Antioch where he narrowly missed being assassinated by Sallustus, who was a trooper in the *Equites Scutarii* guard unit.[35] Valens meted out terrible punishments to both the innocent and guilty in response to having nearly lost his life to an assassin's blade. Accusations of sorcery reared its head again and many noble men of all stations were accused of crimes linked to such practices and most suffered terrible fates.[36] Whilst Valens appeared to abandon reason in the East, in the West Valentinian, spurred on by Maximinus, was also abusing his power by meting out punishments to both civil and military men for what were in essence fairly trivial matters.[37] The acts committed by those two Emperors were an indication of the two brothers' imperfect natures. On the one hand they could be both fair and wise in their dealings with others, yet, if the circumstances were right, and spurred on by those with other agendas, the unpredictable and rather unpleasant sides to their characters could reveal themselves, to the detriment of many within the Empire.

During AD 372 Valentinian again attempted to deal with Macrianus, King of the Alamanni. Valentinian had learnt from deserters of the location of Macrianus, and he had a pontoon made of boats thrown across the Rhine and sent Severus with the infantry to Mattiacae Aquea (Wiesbaden) where Severus waited for Valentinian and the rest of the army to catch up.[38]

Theodosius and the cavalry under his command were then sent out ahead of the main force, probably to scout the way and ensure no one alerted Macrianus of the coming of the Roman army. The whole venture came to nought as the infantry disobeyed Valentinian's orders to remain quiet in the presence of the enemy. They, when coming upon the site where Macrianus was based, plundered and set fire to the area, alerting the Alamanni to the Romans' presence. The Alamanni warriors managed to prevent Macrianus' capture by spiriting him away in cart and hiding him in the hills. Valentinian ordered the region to be devastated for fifty miles around before returning to his base at Treves. In order to frustrate the designs of Macrianus, Valentinian placed Fraomarius, an Alamannic noble loyal to Valentinian, as King over the Bucinobantes, who were an Alamannic tribe living near to Mainz.[39]

I have already noted above that there were problems in Africa, and another cause of this was the revenge sought by Romanus on Firmus, a Prince of the Moorish people in Africa. Firmus had murdered one of his brothers, Zammac, who was a favourite of Romanus, and Romanus did everything in his power to bring Firmus down, including sending continuous reports of Firmus' alleged wrong-doings to the court of Valentinian.[40] Firmus believed the only way to ensure his safety was to rebel and sought support from the other Moorish peoples. Theodosius was despatched in AD 372 from Arles with auxiliary troops to Africa where he met up with Romanus in Sitifian Mauritania (Setif).[41] Theodosius rebuked Romanus for causing the current problems in Africa and he sent Romanus to take charge of the border defences. Later, after the successful conclusion of his campaign against Firmus, Theodosius had both Romanus and his second in command Vincentius arrested for their crimes. When Firmus learnt of the arrival of Theodosius and his army he sent envoys with a letter explaining his side of the story.[42] At first it appeared as if Theodosius looked favourably on this as he accepted hostages and gave an indication he was willing to accept peace between them. Theodosius then went to Pancharia to ostensibly inspect the legions stationed there, but in reality he was preparing them for war.[43] He then returned to Sitifis where he gathered a combined army of the troops he had brought over from Europe and troops raised from the local tribes, and then began his campaign against Firmus. Theodosius marched to Tubusuptum, near Mount Ferratus, where Firmus sent a second delegation but Theodosius refused this one as no hostages accompanied it as had previously been agreed. Theodosius then shortly afterwards met in battle two of Firmus' brothers, Dius and Mascizel, who were leading the tribes of the Tyndenses and the Masinissenses, and defeated them.[44] The victorious Theodosius destroyed the nearby estate of Petrensis, that belonged to another of Firmus' brothers, and captured the town of Lamfoctum, which he made a base for his food stores. Mascizel, having escaped capture, attacked the Romans again with a hastily raised force and was again routed in battle and barely escaped Theodosius' men.[45] After this disaster Firmus resorted to a novel approach. He sent hostages along with Christian priests to sue for peace. This delegation was accepted by Theodosius and such were the promises given that Firmus himself came to Sitifis and prostrated himself before Theodosius, begging for forgiveness and pardon. This being granted to Firmus, that same Prince left some of his relatives as hostages with Theodosius. Firmus himself went away and returned two days later to the town of Icosium where he gave back not only those prisoners he had captured since the beginning of his revolt but also all the Roman standards, booty and the *Coronam Sacerdotalem* (Priestly Crown that was worn by the high priest of that province).[46]

Theodosius then led his army against the Mazices, a tribe that had sided with Firmus. The Mazices gave up without a fight and Theodosius was then able to enter the city of Caesarea which had been abandoned and neglected. On arrival Theodosius stationed several legions there.[47]

At this point one could be forgiven for thinking that was an end to the revolt and to the problems in Africa, but this was far from the truth. Once word spread of Theodosius' success, various officials, including Vincentius, came from where they had been hiding to Caesarea. He received terrible news from them. Firmus had been stirring up the local tribes in preparation for a further conflict with the Romans. And what was worse, a unit of Roman horse archers, the *Equites Quartae Sagittariorum Cohortis*, and part of an infantry unit, the *Auxilia Palatina Constantiani*, had not only fled to join Firmus, but one of the tribunes of the Constantiani had crowned Firmus with an impromptu diadem. Theodosius induced those units with 'mild punishment' to return back to Roman service and they surprisingly complied, going to the designated town of Tigaviae where Theodosius was waiting. When those units arrived before Theodosius the mild punishment he had promised proved anything but; he allowed the troops under his command to slay the infantry of the Constantiani 'in the old-fashioned way' (probably the old system of decimation where every tenth man in a unit that was chosen for this punishment would be slain by the rest of the army). The fate of the *Quartae Sagittariorum* was different in that Theodosius had the horse archers' officers hands cut off and the rest of the troopers slain. In a similar way Theodosius had a chief and a prefect of the Mazices tribe slain.[48] At this point Theodosius led his army on the offensive against those Moorish tribes who supported Firmus. He spent most of AD 373 hunting Firmus down, in the process fighting a battle against the Mazices' tribe and thoroughly routing them at Castellum Tingitanum, forcing them to accept a Roman pardon, and a promise to support Theodosius.[49] At the town of Adda Theodosius encountered a large army composed of a number of tribes led by Firmus' sister Cyria. Theodosius' army of 3,500 men was no match for the much larger force he faced and he was initially forced to retreat. However, Cyria's armies' pursuit caught Theodosius and his men who were then forced to turn and fight a hasty battle; the Romans would have been slain to a man had not Cyria's army been surprised by the arrival of a combined Roman and Mazices force, throwing Cyria's army into a panic and allowing Theodosius and his surviving men to escape.[50] Theodosius, having reached the town of Tipasa, set about the task of rebuilding his army, sending men 'experienced in persuasion' to most of the surrounding tribes with the intention of bribing or bullying them into entering a treaty. Firmus, learning of this, fled for the safety of the Caprariensian mountains.[51] This allowed Theodosius to attack Firmus' now leaderless and scattered army, easily defeating them, capturing their camp and then placing new leaders over the tribesmen of the country he was moving through. Theodosius set off in pursuit of Firmus once again, easily brushing aside the tribes of the Caprarienses and the Abanni who attacked him near the fortress of Audia, Theodosius learned that the nearby hills were full of enemy tribesmen, which caused him to retreat, further allowing the tribes to gather more reinforcements from the Aethiopians. The combined tribesmen army initially drove Theodosius and his men into headlong retreat. Theodosius recovered his nerves and returned to face the tribesmen in the 'hollow square' formation which allowed him and his army to reach the city of Conta where Firmus had placed all the Roman prisoners he had captured, all of whom were freed by Theodosius and his men.[52]

Theodosius received a report that Firmus had fled to the tribe of the Isaflenses, along with his brother Mazuca and the rest of his surviving family members. Theodosius demanded that tribe to hand over Firmus and his family and when this demand was refused he engaged that tribe in battle, defeated them, and captured Mazuca.[53] Firmus yet again managed to escape capture, whilst Mazuca, badly wounded, died on the way to captivity in Caesarea, only his severed head arriving there as proof of his death. Theodosius pressed his attack on the Isaflenses and conquered them, killing many of that tribe's leaders who had sided with Firmus. Theodosius then marched against the Iubaleni tribe, from whence Firmus' father, Nubel, came. That tribe sought refuge in the local mountains and Theodosius returned back to Audia. Whilst there another tribe, the Iesalenses, approached and offered to side with Theodosius and his army, which was granted.[54]

Theodosius then marched to Medianum where he spent some time resting his men and devising plans for Firmus' capture. Reports reached him that Firmus had made his way back to the tribe of the Isaflenses, where he was sheltered by Igmazen, king of that tribe. Theodosius gathered his army and force marched to engage Igmazen and his tribesmen. Theodosius met with Igmazen, who proceeded to pour a torrent of abuse upon Theodosius before departing. The next day saw Theodosius facing an army of over 20,000 tribesmen, who were also supported by auxiliaries supplied by the Iesalenses who just a short while beforehand had promised to aid Theodosius. Although outnumbered, Theodosius' men fought valiantly, until evening fell when suddenly Firmus appeared on his horse wearing a purple cloak, shouting to Theodosius' men to hand over their leader in exchange for their lives. This caused some of Theodosius men to desert, only the darkness of night allowing Theodosius and the rest of his army to retreat to the fortress of Duodia. He beat off a night attack by the tribesmen and the next day, instead of remaining holed up, he marched his army with great speed out of Duodia to the land of the Iesalenses where he wreaked a terrible revenge on that traitorous tribe. After this he marched all the way back to Sitifis, where he had originally landed in Africa, to replenish his troops and deal with Martinianus and Castor, who were associates of Romanus.[55]

Once rested and replenished, Theodosius again marched against Igmazen and the Isaflenses. Theodosius' attack was so successful that Igmazen not only fled the battlefield, leaving his tribesmen to be slaughtered, but he secretly made his way to Theodosius' camp where he conspired with Theodosius and Masilla, a chieftain of the Mazices tribe, to not only wear down the resolve of the Isaflenses to continue the war, but also allow Igmazen to capture Firmus. The plan was agreed and was entirely successful, Theodosius' constant attacks on the Isaflenses broke that tribe's will to fight and Firmus was captured whilst trying to escape once more and was held captive by Igmazen. Masilla informed Firmus of Igmazen's treachery and in order to prevent being handed over to Theodosius he hanged himself. Igmazen, no doubt fearing the wrath of Theodosius for allowing Firmus to escape justice, took the corpse to Theodosius' camp at the fortress of Subicara where it was paraded before his troops and the local tribesmen in order to prove that indeed Firmus was now dead. Theodosius then returned back to Sitifis where he was greeted like a conquering hero.[56] This episode demonstrated that even when vastly outnumbered Roman armies could defeat their more undisciplined barbarian foes, if led by a competent commander.

Whilst Theodosius was dealing with Firmus' revolt in Africa, the Quadi, a Germanic Tribe who lived north of the Danube and who had been quiet since being dealt with by Constantius II, suddenly erupted in violence against the Romans.[57] The cause of this eruption was due to Valentinian, who, as part of his plan of protecting the frontiers with a string of fortresses, ordered one built across the Danube in the territory of the Quadi. The matter was made worse by Maximinus having his son Marcellianus promoted to the rank of *Dux per Valeriam*, or Duke of the province of Valeria, and then arranging for him to replace Aequitius to take charge of the forts construction.[58] Marcellianus ignored the Quadi's protests until their king, Gabinius, protested in person. Marcellianus' response was to invite Gabinius to a banquet where Marcellianus had Gabinius murdered.[59] This heinous act roused the entire Quadi tribe to murderous indignation and in AD 374 large numbers of them unexpectedly crossed the Danube into Roman territory where they killed many Romans who were at that time busy with the harvest, and those who were not killed were driven back over the Danube along with their animals as prisoners. This act of retribution was almost crowned when the Quadi narrowly missed capturing the soon-to-be wife of Gratian, she only escaping capture by being taken at high speed in a carriage to Sirmium for her safety.[60] The Quadi then allied themselves to their former allies the Sarmatians and the combined horde ravaged widely across the Danube, plundering at will. The barbarian force headed towards Sirmium in Illyricum but discovered that the walls and other defences of that city had been fully repaired under the orders of Probus, the Praetorian Prefect stationed in that city. The Quadi and Sarmatians had no means of taking a city by storm, and frustrated at being unable to do so, they set off in pursuit of Aequitius who they mistakenly blamed for the murder of Gabinius. Two legions, the Pannonica and the Moesiaca (presumably the *Legio Palatina Pannoniciani seniores* and the *Legio Palatina Moesiaci seniores*), were sent to assist Aequitius. Unfortunately those two units quarrelled and in the resultant confusion the Sarmatians attacked the Mosiaca, killing many of them, and then charged and broke through the Pannoniciani, routing both legions in the process.[61] The son of Theodosius, himself called Theodosius, who was at that time *Dux Moesiae*, or Duke of Moesia, and who was soon to become the future emperor known as Theodosius the Great, was despatched to deal with the Sarmatians. He defeated all those tribesmen who had crossed into Roman territory in a number of battles and crossed over the Danube to deal with the rest. Theodosius' campaign against the Sarmatians was so successful that the Sarmatians were forced to beg for peace, which was granted, and they remained quiet for a long time afterwards, especially when troops from Gaul were moved into Illyricum as a deterrence.[62]

Over in the East, a plot was hatched against Pap, King of the Armenians. One of the ringleaders was Terentius, at that time a Dux, he conspired with the 'Gentiles' to bring accusations to Valens of extreme cruelty by Pap against his subjects, and other falsehoods.[63] Valens, believing the accusations, summoned Pap under the pretext of wanting to discuss matters of State. However, once Pap and his escort reached Tarsus he was put under house arrest. At Tarsus Pap learnt that Terentius was advising Valens to appoint a new ruler over Armenia to prevent Armenia falling into the hands of Sharpur, King of the Sassanids.[64] After learning of this plot, Pap fled Tarsus with 300 of his cavalry. Pap and his bodyguard were pursued by one of the legions stationed at Tarsus, who Pap and his men turned and fought, easily routing the legion.[65] Pap rode swiftly East for two days where after some difficulty he managed to escape across the Euphrates with his men. Valens, fearing Pap would now flee to Sharpur, sent 1,000 archers under the command of the General Danielus, and also Barzimeres, a Tribune of the *Equites Scutarii* (a guard cavalry unit that Barzimers was presumably leading) to bring back Pap. This force managed to overtake Pap and his men, who had made slow progress due to the unfamiliarity of the country they were travelling through. Danielus set up an ambush on the two roads Pap would have to take through the rough terrain in that region, so that no matter what road Pap took he and his men would face an ambushing force. However, the ambush failed due to the ambushing troops being seen by a traveller who, taking a path between the two roads, was captured by Pap's men who led him before Pap where he told that king what he had seen. Pap despatched a rider down both roads with an order to secure accommodation for Pap, which was really a ruse to fool the Roman ambushing force should any of the riders be captured. The traveller led Pap and his men back along the path between the roads where they then made their escape back to Armenia where the Armenian people greeted him with open arms.[66]

Danielus and Barzimeres returned empty handed to Tarsus where they were berated for letting Pap escape. They concocted a story that Pap had used magic to transform both himself and his men into unrecognizable forms, wrapping themselves in a cloak of darkness and so evaded capture. Valens, ever roused to anger by these kinds of accusations, discussed ways of finally dealing with Pap. It was agreed that Trajanus, who was now in charge of the military forces in Armenia, should deal with Pap. This general, taking a lead from how King Gabinus was dealt with, lured Pap to a lunch in his honour. Trajanus excused himself during the meal to supposedly relieve himself and taking this as the signal to act, one of the Germanic guards attending Trajanus without warning attacked Pap with his sword. Pap attempted to defend himself with a dagger but he was no match for his assailant and he was brutally slain.[67]

The ramifications of the murder of Pap would make itself felt during the years just before Adrianople, and will be discussed in Chapter Nine.

Valentinian, learning what had happened in Illyricum, made preparations to march to that province to deal with the Quadi and their Sarmatian allies;

this was in the autumn of AD 374. However, he was persuaded to wait until the following spring due to both the fact that the weather would not be conducive for setting on campaign late in the year, and also because there were still threats from the Germanic tribes north of Gaul that needed to be resolved. Valentinian agreed to stay and deal with the Alamanni King Macrianus in a way that was advantageous to both parties. Accordingly a meeting was agreed at the city of Mogonticum (modern Mayence) on the bank of the Rhine. Macrianus arrived at the appointed date and time on the north bank with a large number of warriors. Valentinian was conveyed over by boat in a scene very reminiscent of Valens' meeting with Athanaricus in their meeting on the Danube. Speeches were made and an oath of friendship was taken by both leaders, Macrianus becoming a loyal ally to the Romans to the end of his days. Valentinian then retired to Trier for the winter.[68]

In the spring of AD 375 Valentinian set out from Trier to finally deal with the Sarmatians and their allies the Quadi. Whilst making his way to Illyricum a deputation from the Sarmatians met him and begged Valentinian for peace, stating that they had nothing to do with the incursions the previous year. Valentinian informed them that he would make proper investigation on his arrival in Illyricum and he proceeded to the abandoned town of Carnuntum in Illyricum where he set up his headquarters.[69] He spent several months building up his army and supplies in readiness for an attack on the Quadi. During that time he was involved in several intrigues but did nothing either to investigate the murder of King Gabinius or to punish anyone involved in that act and other crimes.[70] Once preparations were ready Valentinian sent Merobaudes and Count Sebastianus with an army to attack the territory of the Quadi, Valentinian himself with the rest of the army crossed the Danube near Acincum (modern Ofen) on a temporary bridge. The Quadi, having moved away from the area Merobaudes and Sebastianus were attacking were unexpectedly attacked by Valentinian's force.[71] The Quadi scattered and the survivors hid themselves in the hills. Having done this, and not being able to flush the remaining Quadi from their hiding places, Valentinian returned to Acincum where he began to look for suitable winter quarters. He made for Bregitio (modern Szoeny) by force marching along the bank of the Danube and set up his quarters there. Whilst at Bregitio various portents were seen in the West that would afterwards be interpreted as foretelling the death of

Valentinian. They included a number of comets seen in the sky, a thunderbolt hit Sirmium setting fire to the Palace, Senate and Forum; an owl was seen perched on the roof of the Imperial baths at Savaria, whilst the night before his death Valentinian had a vision of his wife in mourning attire.[72] The morning after the vision of his wife Valentinian was approached by envoys from the Quadi who begged for his forgiveness and for peace, offering to give recruits for the Roman army and other promises. Unfortunately the manner of the Quadi envoy during their plea sent Valentinian into a rage; such was the fury of it that it triggered a stroke from which he did not recover. Shortly after being led away by his attendants he died on 18 November AD 375 at the age of 55.[73] This one event, amongst so many others that drove nails into the heart of the Empire, was to prove the most devastating as now Valens, who had tended to bend to his brother's will, had no such constraints, and Valentinian's influence would be sorely missed in the years leading up to the battle of Adrianople itself.

The death of Valentinian almost led to a power crisis. Gratian, Valentinian's son who had been promoted to the title of Caesar and who was next in line to take up the Imperial power, was back in Trier, and his uncle Valens, who could also have taken sole charge of the empire, was far away in Antioch in the East. To prevent the Gallic troops from raising another to the Purple, Merobaudes, taking stock of the situation, sent Sebastianus, who was the most likely candidate to be elevated to power by the troops and who was at that time unaware of Valentinian's death, as far from the region as possible. Once Valentinian's body was being taken to Constantinople to be interred, Merobaudes arranged for Valentinianus, the 4-year-old son of Valentinian to be brought from where he was staying to Bregitio to Constantinople. Just six days after the death of Valentinian, Valentinianus was clothed in a purple cloak and declared Augustus and to reign as co-emperor of the West with Gratian.[74]

As can be seen in this chapter, the years from AD 367, when Valens was about to embark on his campaigns over the Danube against the Goths, up to AD 376 when the Goths massed on the northern banks of the same river, were very turbulent and there were few months when some sort of crisis did not rear its ugly head. Had not Sharpur intervened in Armenia then it's highly likely that Valens would have been far more successful against

Athanaricus and his Goths as he would not have had to despatch part of his campaigning army East under Arintheus. The forces despatched East from AD 371 would have weakened the Northern provinces facing the Danube frontier, and that would also have impacted on the ability of the Romans to deal with the upcoming crisis in AD 376. These events have not been fully considered by those who have studied Valens' Gothic campaigns and the Battle of Adrianople itself. The impact of the almost incessant warfare from AD 367 onwards would have meant that resources that could have been put towards dealing a fatal blow to the Goths had to be used elsewhere.

However, the one event for me that would prove deadly to the Roman state was the death of Valentinian. Valentinian's death would be a most devastating blow, one that would not be appreciated at the time. It allowed Valens unbridled reign over the East as he would no longer have to seek approval from his much more able brother for any future actions. He would instead rely on his court officials and military officers for advice, and that advice would ultimately lead to Valens' downfall.

Chapter Seven

AD 376 – The Beginning of the End

When Valens woke up on the morning of the first day of the year AD 376 he would have had no idea how that year was going to change not only his life, his reign over the Roman Empire, but also the far more dramatic consequences for the Roman Empire as a whole. It cannot be underestimated that what was going to occur during this fateful year would do to the Empire, for just 100 years later one half of the Roman Empire would no longer exist, and the other half would increasingly rely on Goths and other 'barbarians' to protect their borders.

There were indications to the citizens of the Empire that the year AD 376 was going to be a turbulent one. At the end of AD 375 various signs and portents were seen throughout the eastern provinces that were taken as predicting something dire was going to occur to Valens. The people of Antioch rioted and many chanted for Valens to be burned alive. The baths Valens had built in that city were torched; this was taken as a sign that this too would be the fate Valens would suffer in the future. The ghosts of Pap and the others Valens had condemned to death were seen to roam abroad 'shrieking horrible songs at night, in the form of dirges, tormented many with dire terrors'. And when the walls of Chalcedon were being demolished at Valens' command a stone block was revealed that had this inscription written in Greek on its surface:

When gaily through the city's festal streets
Shall whirl soft maidens in a happy dance,
When mournfully a wall shall guard a bath,
Then countless hordes of men spread far and wide
With warlike arms shall cross clear Istrus' stream
To ravage Scythia's fields and Mysia's land.
But mad with hope when they Pannonia raid,
There battle and life's end their course shall check.

These verses were to be later interpreted as signalling the coming of the Huns and the crossing of the Danube by the Goths.[1]

At the end of Chapter Five we saw that the Goths had elected a new leader, Alavivus, and had agreed to move south-west towards the Danube with the intention of crossing over and settling in Thrace. Once on the northern bank of that river Alavivus sent an envoy to Valens, asking Valens' permission for the Goths to be allowed to cross the Danube and settle in Thrace, and in return the Goths 'would not only lead a peaceful life but would also furnish auxiliaries, if circumstances required'.[2] Rumours had already swept through the Empire of troubles and warfare beyond the Danube, which was of a scale unheard of before. Tales of a terrifying new race who were the instigators behind this conflict also began to circulate. The Gothic envoys cemented the rumours into something concrete and real. Valens was swayed by the council of those at his court, who said that the coming of the Goths was a stroke of good fortune. They persuaded Valens that the Goths would provide him with willing recruits to swell the ranks of the eastern army, saving him the expense of raising recruits from the provinces who would have had to have been paid for otherwise.[3] Valens duly despatched officials with carts to transport the Goths to their new homeland in Thrace, once they had crossed over the Danube. There were so many Goths massed on the far bank that it took days to transport them over, using boats, rafts and even hollowed out tree-trunks. Some, fearing to either be left behind or to be attacked by the rapidly approaching Huns, chanced swimming across and many drowned as a result.[4] Alavivus, now joined by Fritigern, was warmly received by Valens who gave orders that the Goths should receive both food and lands to cultivate. Had this command been adhered to then it is likely the course of history would have been changed. Commanding the disarming of the Goths once they had crossed may also have prevented disaster striking. However, the two men sent with the army to oversee the transition of the Goths from the Danube to their new homelands so bungled the affair that the Goths rose up in an armed rebellion. Count Lupicinus, Commander of the army in Thrace, and his colleague Duke Maximus, abused the Goths under their charge. Instead of giving the Gothic refugees decent food to eat, they instead gave orders for all the dogs that were in the region to be gathered up and then each one was to be exchanged for a Goth. These Goths were then enslaved, and some of these poor devils were the sons of chieftains.[5] To add to this insult, Viderichus, the boy King of the Greuthungi Goths, having arrived on the north bank of the Danube in the company of Farnobius, Alatheus and Saphrax, sent envoys to Valens to ask to be received like Fritigern and Alavivus had been. These envoys were rejected and the Greuthungi were forced to stay beyond the Roman frontier.[6] Athanaricus also made his appearance on the banks of the Danube. He, on hearing that Viderichus and the Greuthungi had been refused entry, suddenly remembered that he had forced Valens in to signing a rather humiliating peace treaty in the middle of that river. Fearing Valens would perhaps not take this too kindly, he declared his vow to never set foot on Roman soil and retreated to Caucalanda, where his men drove out the Sarmatians who lived there.[7]

The Tervingi Goths grew ever more restive and angry as Lupicinus and his cohort Maximus made the most out of the plight of those tribesmen. Finally Lupicinus recognized that his actions were rousing the Goths into anger and he sent troops to send the Goths as quickly as possible to their allotted place within the Empire. In the rush and confusion to speed up the transition of the Goths across the Danube, the Greuthungi, still camped on the north bank of the Danube, saw an opportunity to make their own crossing over the river whilst the troops and boats that were stationed there to prevent their crossing were now being tasked with moving on the Tervingi. This they did completely unopposed and they pitched their camp a little distance from Fritigern's.[8]

Fritigern made contact with the Greuthungi who had now crossed the Danube, and then in company with them, he made his way slowly to the city of Marcianople where both he and Alavivus had been summoned by Valens.[9] And it was at Marcianople that the final act that led to the rebellion of the Goths took place. Lupicinus invited both Alavivus and Fritigern to a dinner in their honour, which in itself should have put those two leaders on guard, knowing the Roman penchant for dealing with their barbarian guests at such occasions! Lupicinus had his troops refuse the rest of Goths entry into the city, despite the Goths reminding them that they had been received into the empire in friendship and they needed to enter the city to obtain food. A quarrel arose between the inhabitants of the city and the Goths attempting to gain entry which quickly broke out into deadly violence.

Lupicinus received word of what was happening outside the city and he ordered Alavivus' and Fritigern's attendants and guards, who were waiting outside the room whilst their leaders were eating, to be put to death. The Goths outside the walls were made aware of this treacherous act and, fearing that their leaders were going to suffer a similar fate, began to mass against the city walls and uttered dire threats towards the inhabitants unless their leaders were set free. Fritigern, quickly assessing the situation, demanded to be allowed to go with Alavivus to their people to prove they were still alive, and that would in turn calm their fellow tribesmen down. This was agreed to and when the Goths outside the walls saw their leaders still alive they began to loudly rejoice. Taking full advantage of the confusion, Fritigern and Alavivus found horses and quickly rode away, setting in motion the war that was soon to come. When word of the Roman treachery reached the rest of the Tervingi they became enraged, raising their standards, and blowing their horns, signalling that they were now at war with Rome. With that rallying call Gothic raiding parties spread out through Thrace to pillage and plunder it. Lupicinus reacted to this dangerous situation by gathering together all his forces at Marcianople and rushed to meet the Goths nine miles outside the city. The Goths, not waiting for the Romans to get into battle formation, fell on Lupicinus' army and overran it, capturing all the standards and donning the arms and armour of the fallen Roman troops. Lupicinus fled the scene of the battle whilst his men were still fighting and made for the safety of Marcianople, leaving his men to die.[10]

Word of the Gothic rebellion quickly spread, and when the news reached Adrianople another outbreak of Gothic violence occurred. Sometime beforehand Valens had received two other Gothic chieftains, Colias and Sueridus, and had allowed them, with their tribesmen, to spend the winter at Adrianople. At first those two chieftains took little notice of the reports of their fellow tribesmen's revolt, their main concern being the welfare of their people within the city. This was soon to change when they were unexpectedly presented by a letter from Valens ordering them to go to Hellespontus in Asia Minor. The two chieftains were willing to comply, but first they requested food and money for the journey and a stay of two days, presumably to allow their tribesmen to make themselves ready for the journey. The chief magistrate of the city, who was already angry with the Goths due to them plundering his suburban villa that was beyond the city walls, armed some of the citizens and with them descended upon the Goths within the walls. The citizens brandished their weapons and made threats against the Goths, issuing demands that the Goths leave immediately. The Goths were stunned at this turn of events and refused to move, but when the armed mob before them resorted from hurling abuse, to then hurling missiles at them, the Goths reacted by attacking the mob, killing many and putting the rest to flight.[11] The Goths stripped the fallen of their arms, leaving them armed and armoured on an equal basis to their Roman enemies, and they left the city. They soon fell in with Fritigern and his tribesmen who were camped not far off. This combined horde then laid siege to Adrianople. Unfortunately the Goths were both ill-prepared for and inexperienced in that kind of warfare, losing many men to the slingshot and arrows from the defenders on the walls. Fritigern, seeing how ineffective his men were at besieging a city, called off the attack and uttered these famous words to his men, that he 'kept peace with walls'; he sent the bulk of them to plunder the area around the city, just leaving a small force behind to prevent the defenders of Adrianople undertaking any rash action.[12]

Once news of the revolt at Adrianople reached the ears of the other Goths scattered throughout Thrace they came rapidly to Fritigern's camp, swelling the ranks of his horde. And not only Goths came to him, disaffected Romans too flocked to Fritigern's banner. These deserters proved very useful to Fritigern, and extremely disastrous to the Empire, as they were able to show the Goths hidden stores of grain, less frequented pathways and the hiding places of citizens who had taken refuge in the countryside. Many were captured and dragged off into captivity by the Goths, age and sex did not seem to matter, such was the fate of those who were unable to resist.[13]

Some interesting points need to be examined here. The first one that demands attention is why didn't the Romans who were ferrying the Goths across the Danube disarm them before they reached the other side? This is surely the one thing anyone with even an ounce of sense should have done to ensure that if the Goths became restive then at least they could have been relatively easily overpowered by the smaller yet better armed Romans supervising them. Yet, it is quite apparent that this did not happen as commentators at the time lamented. Another interesting fact was that

Goths were already in residence in the Empire before Alavivus and Fritigern had crossed the Danube, because, as I noted above, Colias and Sueridus were already stationed in Adrianople with their fellow tribesmen. This may well be due to the fact that Valens had begun actively recruiting from the Goths for his proposed invasion of Sassanid Persia, which was as a direct result of the Sassanid interference in Armenia. We will read later in this book that other Goths were stationed much further East for that very same reason. One last point intrigues me the most. After escaping for his life with Alavivas, Fritigern then camped a short distance outside of Adrianople, and there is little evidence he moved very far from the vicinity of that city during the following two years before the Battle of Adrianople itself. Which begs the question: why? Was it that Fritigern really intended to take up Valens' offer to cultivate lands in Thrace? Was he actually sticking to his side of the bargain as much as he could do so, because he still had a debt owing to Valens due to the support that Emperor had given to him against Athanaricus? Was Fritigern hoping that the situation could still be resolved peacefully? If this was indeed the case then subsequent events would put paid to that rather vain hope.

Chapter Eight

The Battle of the Willows

A Blueprint for Disaster?

As the Gothic revolt started to spread, Valens' reaction was to send forces to Thrace to deal with the matter in typical Roman fashion, by making the Goths submit by force of arms. The major battle that ensued should have alerted Valens to how dangerous a foe the Goths truly were.

Valens was still in Antioch when the news of the disaster in Thrace reached him. At first the news totally threw him; without warning, the Goths, who just a short while before had been friends to the Romans, were now pillaging and plundering the very province Valens had given them permission to settle in. To his credit, Valens acted swiftly, he sent Victor, now *Magister Equitum*, to the court of Sharpur to discuss what to do about Armenia.[1] If the negotiations proved favourable Valens would then be able to withdraw troops from Armenia that had been stationed there to guard against Sassanid incursions and move them to the trouble zone. Victor's negotiations did indeed prove successful, and Valens made preparations to leave Antioch and travel to Constantinople, but before he did so he sent the aged generals, Profuturus and Trajanus to Thrace with some of the legions that had been stationed in Armenia, and who were now free to march due to Victor's success. These two generals, on reaching the area around Mount Haemus, found a large band of Goths, and immediately launched an attack on them. The attack drove the Goths beyond those mountains and into canyons from which they could not escape. The Romans initially intended to keep the Goths penned in and to starve them into submission, this was to be assisted by the aid of reinforcements comprised of auxiliary troops led by another general, Frigeridus.[2]

Frigeridus had been sent by Gratian, Emperor of the West to aid Valens. Gratian also sent one of his most able generals, Richomeres, who was at that time *Comes Domesticii*, or Commander of the Household troops, the Emperor's personal guard, with some under-strength units to aid Valens.[3] Before Frigeridus could deal with the Goths he suddenly fell ill and it was agreed that Richomeres would take command of not only Frigeridus' troops, but also those of Trajanus and Profuturus. These last two generals were by now camped near a town called Ad Salices, ('By the Willows'). The reason they were there was due to the Roman scouts having discovered a large band of Goths camped near to that town. The Goths were sheltering behind one of their wagon laagers which they had drawn up in a circle, like a wall, behind which they stood in apparent safety.[4] At this point Richomeres appeared to be content just to keep the Goths under constant observation, and if it looked like they were going to attempt to break camp and move off, then the plan would be to attack the rear of the Gothic wagon column and kill as many of the Goths as possible. Whilst sound, this plan ultimately failed as the Goths, informed by Roman deserters from Richomeres' army, decided to stay put and remain camped where they were. The Goths behind the wagons sent messengers out to the other Gothic bands that were plundering the local countryside, requesting them to come and aid their brethren who were besieged behind the wagons. Large numbers of Goths responded to the call and made their way from the local countryside to the wagon laager, swelling both the number of the defending Goths, and boosting their morale and their willingness to fight. In fact so many came to the encampment that a large proportion had to camp outside of the wagons.[5] The Gothic chieftains, judging the mood and sentiments of the Goths, both behind the wagons and those camped outside of them, agreed it was now time for action. A long night descended upon both Goths and the Romans who were still camped some distance off, both sides' warriors barely sleeping, the Goths because they were now fired up and eager for battle, the Romans because they knew the coming dawn would see them battle a foe that substantially outnumbered them.[6]

Dawn the following day saw the Goths, after exchanging oaths in their manner, suddenly burst out from their camp to reach some higher ground where they intended to descend upon the Romans below 'like so many rollers'. The Romans foiled this plan by forming ranks and stood their ground rather than advancing into the Gothic trap. Realizing the Romans were not going to fall for their ruse, the Goths on the slopes descended back down. Both the Roman army and the Gothic horde at this point cautiously approached each other. The Gothic warriors and Roman infantry stopped at a distance where hand-hurled missiles could be exchanged, whereupon 'The Romans in unison sounded their war-cry, as usual rising from a low to a louder tone, of which the national name is barritus and thus roused themselves to mighty strength.'[7] The Goths, unperturbed, responded by singing 'the glories of their forefathers with wild shouts'. Ammianus makes an interesting observation at this point of his narrative, in that he noted the 'discordant clamour of different languages' when the Romans and Goths raised their various battle-cries. This was an indication that both within the Roman ranks, and also within those of the Goths, there were warriors from different provinces, tribes, and perhaps even allied nations in the ranks of both armies.

After both sides raised their war cries, their skirmishers clashed, and after the skirmishers withdrew, this was followed by the typical pre hand-to-hand combat missile barrage (see Chapter Fifteen). The Romans then stood firm and locked shields so that they formed a shield wall type formation in preparation to meet the on-rushing Goths. The Goths charged wildly and attempted to break through the Roman line on the Roman left wing by throwing 'huge clubs, hardened in the fire'. This tactic initially worked as this onslaught weakened that point of the Roman line and into it charged the Goths. The Romans on the left flank were unable to contain the Goths who managed to break through the front line and they were only checked by the timely arrival of reserves stationed behind the Roman front line.[8] This enabled the Roman left wing to rally and stabilize and the battle grew in intensity. Missiles of all kinds flew in both directions, javelins, darts, sling stones and arrows all met their mark and those who were not slain by those weapons were then run through by swords and spears. Those who broke ranks and fled were chased down by both side's cavalry who 'slashed at their heads and backs', whilst those who had fallen down in the main battle line were hamstrung by any opposing Roman infantryman or Gothic warrior who came across them. Ammianus gave a graphic account of the whole grisly scene – '... the whole battlefield was covered with corpses, some were lying among them who were mortally wounded, and cherished a vain hope of life; some were smitten with a bullet from a sling or pierced with arrows tipped with iron; the heads of others were split through mid-forehead and crown with swords and hung down on both shoulders, a most horrible sight."[9] The battle raged without quarter and it was only when evening fell and the subsequent darkness covered the battlefield that allowed the men on both sides to break off from combat and return to their respective camps.

Both sides had inflicted terrible losses on each other, and neither the Goths nor the Romans were in any fit state to continue the battle the following day, nor could they prevent any attempt of either party to leave the area. The next morning the Roman commanders took advantage of the situation and returned with their surviving troops to Marcianople. The Goths did not interfere with the retreat of the Romans, in fact they did not venture from their wagons for a whole week.[10] This allowed the Romans to send troops to the Haemus Mountains where they built barriers across the narrow passes in order to prevent the Goths still holed up there from breaking through. They hoped by doing this they would be able to starve the Goths who were trapped behind the barriers into submission. And to aid this tactic all available food and fodder was gathered up and brought to the fortified cities in the region so that even had the Goths managed to break through the barriers and overwhelm the defenders, they would have found nothing to sustain them. Such became the plight of the Goths behind the barriers that they were forced into forming an alliance with their adversaries the Huns and Alans, who were persuaded to join the Goths on the promise of gaining rich rewards if they did so.[11]

The Battle of the Willows has, in my opinion, been rather strangely overlooked by most of the historians who have examined the Battle of Adrianople. Yet the impact of Ad Salices would be felt right up to the Battle of Adrianople itself. Many of the commanders at Ad Salices, plus the surviving troops from that battle, would be present at Adrianople. They would have experienced first-hand how dangerous a foe the Goths were on the battlefield. And they would no doubt have had a certain uneasiness and lack of enthusiasm about having to face a similar Gothic horde in the future. The impact of Ad Salices would be felt not only in the loss of men, but also on the minds of those who were to command at any future battle against the Goths. The effect cannot be underestimated of what must have been a severe shock to the Romans, that a barbarian tribe could force what was in effect a drawn result upon a well-trained Roman army. It did not bode well for any future such battles.

Chapter Nine

The Roman Offensives AD 377–378

The year AD 376 ended with the Romans having failed to deal with the Gothic revolt. All was not lost however, although there had been setbacks such as Ad Salices, even at that battle the Romans had not really suffered a defeat. What was more, the battles that had been fought were not by Roman field armies, instead they had been fought by elements of the field armies. What would happen should an entire field army face the Goths? There was no indication that the following year should not see the Romans victorious, and to this end both Valens, and his nephew Gratian, were gathering their forces to crush the Goths and the other barbarian threats once and for all.

Not long after the Battle of Ad Salices, Valens despatched Saturninus, who was given temporary command of the cavalry, to assist Trajanus and Profuturus with the blocking operation, Richomeres having been recalled back to Gaul on Gratian's orders.[1] When Saturninus learnt that the Huns and Alans had now joined with the Goths he gathered together all the troops watching and guarding the passes and he ordered them to retreat. Saturninus no doubt feared that the by now starving and desperate warriors behind the barriers would be forced to storm the barriers and in turn overwhelm the Roman defenders. Whilst this action would have led to the Roman troops being led to safety, it allowed the combined Gothic, Hunnic and Alan horde to freely move out of the mountains through the now undefended passes and defiles. This murderous mob burst out of the mountains and ravaged Thrace from the Danube to the Rhodope, and even travelled down as far as the Hellespont.[2] They captured the rich and poor alike, driving them into captivity. The barbarian horde then made for the town of Dibaltum where they surprised a troop of the Scutarii Cavalry and an Auxilia Palatina unit, the Cornuti, led by the Tribune Barzimeres, who, along with other troops, were about to pitch camp for the night. A battle broke out between the

Romans and the horde, the Romans were holding their own and it looked like they could last out until nightfall, which would have allowed the Romans to be able to retreat. But the sudden appearance of a large number of enemy cavalry put paid to any chance of the Romans escaping; the unfortunate Romans were surrounded and cut to pieces, Barzimeres falling alongside his men.[3]

After the victory at Dibaltum the Goths learnt that Gratian had despatched Frigeridus with troops to aid his Uncle Valens. Frigeridus was at a fortress he had constructed in Thrace, at a place called Beroea. The Goths, recognizing the threat that Frigeridus and his men posed, rushed as quickly as they could with the Hun and Alan mercenaries to Beroea where they hoped to catch Frigeridus off guard. Fortunately for the Romans, the scouts Frigeridus had sent out for the very purpose of detecting such an action by the Goths, spotted the on-rushing barbarians. This timely warning allowed Frigeridus and his army to march out of the fortress and retire to Illyricum unscathed. After successfully escaping from the Goths in Thrace, Frigeridus then chanced upon the Gothic Chieftain Farnobius and his band of Goths, who were now joined by another Gothic tribe, the Taifali, who had lately been allies of the Romans during the reign of Constantius II. Frigeridus drew up his army in battle formation and launched a devastating attack on Farnobius and his men, killing that chieftain and most of the Goths he had led. The survivors were sent to Italy to work the fields around Parma, Mutina and Regium.[4]

If the troubles in Thrace had been the only problems the Romans were experiencing then there was a very good chance matters could have been settled in the Romans' favour. Unfortunately further troubles were brewing beyond the eastern and western frontiers of the Empire which would not only delay the victory Valens so desperately needed, but would ultimately put paid to any chance of victory over the Goths.

After the death of Pap in Armenia during AD 377, the events of which were discussed in Chapter Six, Sharpur, King of Kings of Sassanid Persia, sent a deputation led by Arraces to Valens' court to negotiate what to do about Armenia. Valens refused both solutions put forward by Sharpur as it would have meant withdrawing all Roman troops in Armenia, practically handing the country on a plate to the Sassanids.[5] Valens instead sent Victor, this time accompanied by Urbicius, *Dux Mesopotamiae*, back to Sharpur with an 'ultimatum in plain language', which in essence demanded that Sharpur keep himself out of Armenia and its affairs. Upon the return of Victor and Urbicius, Sharpur despatched the Surena, who ranked next to Sharpur, to the court of Valens, offering the Romans some minor territories in Armenia as an inducement to agree to Sharpur's terms. However, despite being treated as an honoured guest by Valens, the Surena returned empty-handed.[6] This was the final straw, both Sharpur and Valens had only one last resort, and that was war. Valens' preparations dwarfed those of Julian's, he intended invading Sassanid Persia with a massive force consisting of three armies.[7] To this end he began actively recruiting from those Goths currently not rebelling in Thrace. Sharpur, learning of these preparations, ordered the Surena to not only recover the territories in Armenia that had been handed over to Valens as gifts, but also to attack the Roman troops protecting Sauromaces, the new King of Armenia, who had been appointed to that throne by Valens. The perilous situation in Thrace prevented Valens from acting against the Surena and his forces, and also forced Valens to abandon his invasion so that he could deal with the Gothic problem.[8]

Over in the West, Gratian's preparations to assist his uncle were to receive a setback. The Lentienses, an Alamannic tribe whose territory bordered that of the province of Raetia, learnt from Gratian's armour-bearer, who was a member of that tribe and who had travelled back to his homeland on leave, that Gratian intended marching eastwards to provide support to his uncle Valens. This was too good an opportunity to give up and when the Rhine froze over in February AD 378, so that men and horses could cross it, the Lentienses chose that moment to strike. They had learnt that Gratian was on his way to Illyricum with his army and would be unable to act against them before they could return back to their lands. However, unbeknown to the Lentienses, two crack Auxilia Palatina units, the Celtae and the Petulantes, were camped close to the spot on the Rhine where the Lentienses intended crossing and these units easily beat off the raiders, forcing them back over the Rhine.[9] Despite this setback the Lentienses were determined to take advantage of the fact that Gratian was now far away with his army in Illyricum. They gathered up as many warriors from within their territory as they could, the sources state they numbered between 40,000 and 70,000 strong.[10] With this huge force they crossed the Rhine once more, bent on plundering Raetia. Gratian learnt of this threat just in time, when he received messengers sent by the forces left in Gaul. He recalled the troops he had sent ahead, turned around and marched back to join up with the Gallic army. Gratian handed control of the Gallic army to Nannienus, and he also assigned Mallobaudes, who was not only now *Comes Domesticii* (Commander of the Household troops), but also King of the Franks, to assist in the command of the army. The Gallic army met the Lentienses, led by their King Priarius, at Argentaria. A general engagement broke out and at a critical point in the battle the Roman troops broke off combat, retired a short distance before turning and forming ranks again. The Lentienses, seeing this, became convinced that the Romans were luring them forward into a trap, believing that Gratian had arrived with reinforcements. The Lentienses, fearing being trapped between two Roman armies, themselves broke off from combat and began to flee towards the Rhine. The pursing Romans not only managed to catch and kill Priarius, but also slaughtered most of his tribe, only 5,000 of those who fought at that battle managed to make it back to their homelands.[11] If they thought Gratian was now done with them they were very much mistaken. Gratian, hearing about the Gallic army's victory over the Lentienses, crossed the Rhine with his own army and entered their homeland. The Lentienses were in no position to put up any resistance and on hearing of Gratian's approach they gathered up their wives and children, and took to the mountains. Gratian ordered 500 of the most experienced men in each legion to be detached and these troops, along with the imperial guard, were sent up the mountains after the remaining Lentienses. The Lentienses beat off the Roman assault during a day long battle, forcing Gratian to call off the attack. Gratian then resorted to laying siege to those cowering in the heights above him. The Lentienses foiled this tactic by moving along the mountain range, but when they learnt Gratian's army was still pursing them they appealed for mercy and surrendered. Gratian granted them fairly lenient terms and they returned to their homeland. Gratian, after severely punishing the armour-bearer who had caused so much harm in the first place, resumed his march East. Gratian replaced Frigeridus with another *Comes* called Maurus, who was by no means as capable a general as Frigeridus was.[12] Why Gratian replaced Frigeridus at such a critical time is a mystery. The only answer could be that Gratian was worried that Frigeridus would take advantage of his going East and then make a play for imperial power. Packing Frigeridus off into retirement and replacing him with someone who would not inspire the troops to promote him above his station may have appeared prudent at the time. Too many times in the past, when a crisis arose from across the borders, there were those only too willing to seize their chance and become a usurper. Now was not the time for Gratian to be heading towards a warzone with a potential rival lurking behind him!

Valens meanwhile finally left Antioch and made for Constantinople, where within a few days of his arrival a riot broke out. The cause of this appears to have been the population of that city's exasperation with what they perceived as Valens' laxity in dealing with the Goths, some of whom were at that very time plundering the outlying suburbs of the city.[13] Valens had to act and act fast; he removed Trajanus as commander of the infantry and replaced him with Sebastianus, a much more able and vigorous man who had recently left Gratian's command at his own request to join Valens' army.[14] Once this had been completed, Valens travelled to the imperial villa at Melanthias, some fifteen miles from Constantinople, with the aim of rallying the troops stationed there and using them in his campaign against the Goths. Having achieved that aim he marched with those troops west along the Constantinople to Adrianople road to a military station called Nike. On arrival at Nike Valens received a report from his scouts that the Goths who were still camped near to Adrianople were on the move. The Goths, on hearing Valens was marching towards them with a field army, were now preparing to leave as fast as they could with all their plunder, with the intention of making their way to their 'permanent garrison near Beroea and Nicopolis'.[15] Sebastinanus, recognizing that this was a golden opportunity to catch the fleeing Goths at a severe disadvantage, asked for, and was granted, permission to take 300 men from each legion, and with this force he attempted to catch the Goths unawares.[16] Sebastianus made a rapid march to Adrianople, where initially the inhabitants of that city barred the gates and refused him entry, fearing he had sided with the Goths and was coming not as a protector but as an enemy. After much persuasion he was allowed to enter with his troops where they were given food and allowed to rest for the night. The following day Sebastianus and his men left the city 'in secret haste' and by that evening they were approaching the River Hebrus (now the modern Tonzos in Turkey) where they chanced upon the Goths who just a few days before had fled from the vicinity of Adrianople and who were flying towards their base in Beroea. Sebastianus took advantage of the terrain to remain hidden until nightfall when he led his men stealthily to where the Goths were sleeping by the river. The Goths, totally unaware that they had been pursued from Adrianople, had not set up any pickets and were utterly surprised by Sebastianus' attack. The assault was both unexpected and brutal, only a handful of Goths escaped the carnage to flee to safety across the river. In one fell stroke Sebastianus and his men had not only annihilated a much superior force, but they recaptured 'countless booty, which was too great to be contained in the city (Adrianople) and the broad plain about it'.[17]

Fritigern, who was still camped not far from Adrianople, received news of this disaster from survivors of the attack. He realized that unless he could gather up all the Gothic bands that were out pillaging into a single force, there was a risk each band could be similarly attacked and be picked off one by one by Sebastianus' army. He therefore sent out orders for all the Goths to gather near to the town of Kabyle. Once the Goths had gathered as a group at that location they were led out by Fritigern to 'the open plains', a plan which he hoped would prevent any further surprise attacks upon the Gothic horde.[18]

Gratian meanwhile, having dealt with the Alamanni, now turned his attention to the situation facing Valens in the East. He sent his baggage train on ahead by land whilst he himself sailed down the Danube with a picked force and he entered Sirmium where he rested for four days. He then travelled down the Danube to the Camp of Mars in Moesia where a bout of fever and an attack by a group of Alans delayed his progress.[19]

The events of the coming few days would prove to be crucial not only for Valens and the Goths, but also for the Empire as a whole.

Chapter Ten

The Calm Before the Storm

The Last Fateful Days Before the Battle of Adrianople, the Decisions Made and Why

The situation between the Goths and Valens had reached its most critical point, and the decisions made now would have far reaching consequences for all those involved.

There appears to be some confusion within the text of the usually reliable history of Ammianus at this point. In the previous chapter I discussed how Valens had replaced Trajanus with the more able Sebastinanus and had marched from Melanthias to the 'station of Nice' (Nike). However, Ammianus, when describing the events after Sebastinanus' successful attack on the Goths near Adrianople, had Valens marching once again from Melanthias with '… a force made up of varying elements, but one neither contemptible, nor unwarlike; for he had joined with them also a large number of veterans, among whom were other officers of high rank and Trajanus, shortly before a commander-in-chief, whom he had recalled to active service'.[1] Either Ammianus was confusing earlier events or the implication here was that once Valens had despatched Sebastianus and his 2,000 men to deal with the Goths fleeing from the vicinity of Adrianople, he returned back to Melanthias to gather reinforcements or replacements for the troops under Sebastianus' command. He also recalled Trajanus from retirement, reappointed that former general as *Magister* of the Army and then marched once more back along the Constantinople to Adrianople road towards Adrianople itself. This appears the most logical reading of the text at this point and seems perfectly reasonable under the circumstances previously described in Chapter Nine.

Valens may have been motivated to gather further troops and then march against the Goths for more personal reasons. He was made aware, from regular reports from messengers, of the victories of Gratian and Sebastinanus, both of whom had inflicted crushing defeats upon their respective foes. Valens may have been envious of those two able men's exploits and quite possibly wanted to emulate their exploits, or he had been persuaded by flatterers at the Court that he should ignore advice to return to Constantinople, where he would remain safe, and go and deal with Fritigern and the Goths in person.[2] Either way Valens was now on the move.

Valens received reports from his scouts that the Goths were preparing to block the roads the Roman supply train would need to travel on and to this end in order to frustrate the Gothic plan he sent some infantry archers along with a '*turma*' of cavalry to block the passes the Goths would need to travel through. The same scouts also reported that the main Gothic band, now led by Fritigern, numbered only some ten thousand men in total, was only some fifteen miles from Adrianople and was heading for Nike. Valens, swayed by this report, became determined to march as quickly as possible to Adrianople where he would join Sebastinanus and his men and wait for the arrival of Gratian, where with their combined armies they would be able deal a devastating blow to Fritigern and his horde.[3]

It's worth examining the journey Valens made from Melanthias. The distance from Melanthias to Adrianople was approximately 130 miles. Using Vegetius' rate of march of twenty miles in five summer hours, this should have taken Valens' army just less than a week to march to Adrianople at this speed. As it was likely Valens would have force marched on at least part of the route, as he was in some haste, this may then have increased the distance he had travelled. It would further explain the passage in Ammianus where he makes specific mention of Valens being three days into the march from Melanthias when he received the reports from his scouts that the Goths were now moving past Adrianople on their way to Nike.[4] When Valens received this report he ordered the army to form the 'square formation', a defensive one used when marching through hostile territory, and he hastened with his troops to Adrianople itself. If Valens and his army force-marched part of the way then the journey may have taken only four days in total from Melanthias to Adrianople in this case. On arrival at that city Valens had his men make an encampment of a 'rampart of stakes, surrounded by a moat' and he waited there somewhat impatiently for the arrival of Gratian and the Gallic army.[5] Whilst he was waiting, Richomeres arrived with some troops.

He had been despatched by Gratian not only with an advance party but also Richomeres bore a personal letter for Valens. The letter informed Valens that Gratian was on the march again and would be at Adrianople soon. The letter that Richomeres bore from Gratian also asked Valens to wait patiently for his arrival and 'to not rashly expose himself alone to serious perils'.[6] How far away Gratian was by this time is not known but he must have been less than a week's march away from Adrianople. The basis of my stating this is that Gratian was marching as quickly as possible and we last heard of him was when he was in Moesia at the Camp of Mars, some 370 miles from Adrianople, and that was at least a week before Richomeres arrived with his letter.[7] After reading the letter, Valens called a council of all his high ranking officers to discuss what course of action to take. Ammianus stated that Sebastinanus urged Valens to offer battle against the Goths as soon as possible, whilst Victor, now *Magister Equitum* (Commander of the Cavalry), despite being a Sarmatian by birth and naturally inclined to rashness, with the support of Richomeres and others, counselled waiting instead for Gratian and the Gallic army, so that the combined strength of both armies would overwhelm Fritigern and his Goths.[8]

Unfortunately Sebastinanus, aided by the Court flatterers, won the day, using the argument that he, Sebastianus, had already shown how the Goths could be defeated, and anyway, Valens' army already outnumbered that of Fritigern's by a wide margin, if the reports of the scouts putting Fritigern's band at only 10,000 strong were accurate and true.[9] The Roman confidence in their ability to defeat the Goths is telling. The size of Valens' army is unknown; no existing history gives even a vague figure. However, my own calculation would set it at between 30,000–40,000 strong. We know that Sebastianus took 300 men from each legion when Valens first left Melanthias, and if Zosimus was correct in stating that this force totalled 2,000 men, then there were at least 7 legions in Valens' army at that stage (300 x 7 = 2,100, just a tad more than Zosimus' figure). When Valens returned to Melanthias it's highly likely that he would have gathered more men, and his army may well have contained not only the original seven legions but several more. To this we must add troops that were already in Adrianople plus those that arrived with Richomeres. As many as ten legions could have been present when Valens arrived at Adrianople, with probably the same number of Auxiliary units. This total would put the number of infantry at approximately 30,000 strong, let alone the cavalry of all types that would have been present, which may well have pushed the total size of the army to nearer 40,000 strong. It's no wonder that Valens was confident of victory (see Chapter Fifteen for my discussion on the Late Roman field army sizes).

Whilst the preparations for the coming battle were being made, an envoy sent by Fritigern, consisting of a Christian 'presbyter' (Elder/Priest), accompanied by 'some humble folk' arrived at the Roman camp. The envoy presented Valens with a letter from Fritigern which asked Valens to abide with the Goths' original request when they first arrived on the banks of the Danube some two years ago, i.e. the Goths being allowed to settle in Thrace, and if this was granted, peace would return between the Goths and Romans. The same envoy, a 'confidant and trusted friend of Fritigern', produced another, 'private' letter from Fritigern which stated that in order for Fritigern to 'tame the savagery of his people', and persuade them to agree to peace terms, Valens would need to 'from time to time show them near at hand his army ready for battle'. This show of force from the Romans would then be enough to keep the Goths in check and make sure they stuck to their end of the agreement.[10]

This envoy and the letters he bore are very intriguing and worth examining in some detail. As was discussed in Chapter Five, Fritigern had converted to Christianity as a result of the aid Valens had provided to Fritigern during the civil war between him and Athanaricus. He probably believed that sending a Christian envoy bearing letters, including a personal one would be taken as a sign of his sincerity. And there is evidence to suggest that the contents of both of the letters were in fact not deceptive as Ammianus would have us believe. I believe that they were in fact a sign that Fritigern was making a genuine attempt at ending the conflict with the Romans in a manner that would prove both beneficial and face saving to both sides. Fritigern would have been fully aware that Gratian and the Gallic army were dangerously near. When he arrived the combined armies would have outnumbered his own force by a substantial amount and there would be a very real risk that the Goths would not only face defeat at the hands of the combined army but also risked being enslaved should they be defeated. Fritigern had absolutely nothing to gain by prolonging the conflict, he had no idea that he would be able to defeat a Roman field army; no Gothic horde had faced one so far. He needed the Romans to agree to his terms in order for his people to survive. The part of the private letter that most historians appear to have overlooked that to me shows Fritigern did not want to be attacked and was genuine is where he asked Valens to 'from time to time' make a show of force near to where the Goths planned to settle in Thrace. He did not to require Valens to immediately set off for the Gothic encampment in full battle array. This instead implies that Fritigern was more than happy for Gratian to arrive and then Fritigern could point out to his people that this much more dangerous combined army should be taken note of and an agreement entered into and abided by or face the consequences. Once the Goths had entered into a peace treaty all the Romans needed to do would be to station units at the cities of Adrianople and Marcianople, and every so often send them out on manoeuvres near to the Gothic settlement in Thrace to ensure the peace was maintained. Valens himself also had much to gain if peace terms were agreed even at this late stage. The Goths would no longer be ravaging Thrace, they would not continue to threaten the trade route to Constantinople, and more importantly Valens could send his eastern units back to their stations and then he could set about recruiting from the Goths again for his postponed invasion of Sassanid Persia. The fact that Fritigern had not left the area around Adrianople, and had been in Thrace during the two years since the Goths first crossed the Danube, was also telling. He had not allowed the Goths under his command to move closer to Constantinople or out of Thrace into the surrounding provinces. In fact from all the evidence we have from the surviving histories the vast majority of the Goths were in fact within Thrace between AD 376 and 378, very few ventured outside of that province. It was almost as if they were still complying with the original agreement between themselves and Valens, despite the treatment they had received at the hands of the Romans.

Whatever the intention of Fritigern, Valens sent the envoy back to the Gothic encampment without any agreement being given. The final roll of the dice had been thrown; the events of the following day would forever change Roman history.

Chapter Eleven

9 August AD 378

'The Day the Eagles Fell'

There have been a number of examinations of the Battle of Adrianople, and they all vary in both the quality of their treatment of the battle but also in their interpretation of what actually happened on the battlefield.[1] Apart from Donnelly (2013), there has been little breakdown and analysis of the battle in detail. I have chosen to follow Donnelly's example in this chapter, and I have broken down the battle into distinct parts, using Ammianus as the main source, only using information from the other sources where I feel they add anything relevant or different. This will I believe demonstrate exactly what happened on that day, and why. I will examine the sources for clues as to which direction the Roman army was marching when they left Adrianople, where the army deployed, and where Valens' position on the battlefield was etc. so as to give an indication of the direction the Gothic Cavalry attack came from. Diagram 1 shows the location of Adrianople, now modern Edirne in Turkey with distances marked to the possible sites of the battlefield as noted below. Diagrams 2–5 show how the Gothic wagon laager could have been set up, whilst Diagram 6 shows how I believe the Roman army was formed up, and the direction of the initial Gothic cavalry attack.

And so, on to the fateful day of 9 August AD 378. As we saw in the previous chapter, on 8 August 378 Valens had held a council of war. The outcome of which was that Valens had been persuaded to march out against the Goths the following day. Valens was swayed by the reports from the scouts who had reported that the Goths only numbered 10,000 just a few days beforehand. Most commentators on the battle dispute that, believing that the scouts had underestimated the size of the Gothic horde, because they fail to believe that a 'barbarian' army, possibly a quarter of the size of the Roman army, could possibly defeat the much larger Roman one. But ancient accounts are full of smaller armies defeating ones that substantially outnumbered them, especially if something unexpected happened during the battle.[2] The traditional way of counting how many troops an enemy had was by the scouts undertaking several things. The standards of the enemy army could be counted as they marched by, if you knew how many men were in a unit then the total number of standards that were counted would give you a rough idea of the number of men in the army. Camp fires could also be counted and a rough estimate of the number of men sat around them could be worked out. But in the case of Fritigern's Goths the matter was confused by the Goths moving along not in units but travelling in a wagon train. Yes, you could count the number of wagons and estimate that for every wagon you see there could be probably four people attached to it, and of these four possibly only two may be warriors. So if there were at least 5,000 wagons travelling down from Kabyle that may well have indicated to the Roman scouts that there were only 10,000 Gothic warriors present. However, we know that Fritigern had called for all the Gothic bands in the region to join him, and many of them came without wagons because they had to camp outside of the wagon laager. So, it was entirely possible that instead of 10,000 warriors present there may have been double or more, even perhaps as many as 40,000 warriors, and that included the Gothic cavalry, who were now ominously absent.

Ammianus' account of the day of the battle begins:

But on dawn of that day which is numbered in the calendar as the fifth before the Ides of August (the 09th) the army began its march with extreme haste, leaving all its baggage and packs near the walls of Hadrianopolis with a suitable guard of legions; for the treasury, and the imperial dignity besides, with the (praetorian) prefect and the emperor's council, were kept within the circuit of the walls.

So, according to Ammianus, Valens led his army out of the Roman camp at dawn. The sun rose at approximately 6.00 am at the location of Adrianople (now modern Edirne in north-west Turkey) on 9 August and the army must have been up and ready for the march at least several hours before hand. Valens led the army out in 'extreme haste'. Why? The probability was because Valens did not want the army marching for too long in the very hot temperatures that were likely to occur within a very short time of the sun rising. The temperatures in that region of Turkey regularly reach 40 Celsius (104 degrees Fahrenheit) during the summer months and marching more than a few miles after 6.00 am would have proved extremely uncomfortable, by midday it would have been almost unbearable, especially if the troops had limited access to water. It's unlikely that Valens' haste was due to the concern that the Goths would up camp and move off towards Nike; it's inconceivable that the Goths had not been under constant observation by the scouts, and regular reports about the Goths would have flown back to Adrianople during the night and early morning.

Does Valens leaving the city in haste explain why he left without the baggage train? This is a very important question and a vital clue as to the possible intention of Valens on that day, and one that has been surprisingly overlooked by other commentators of the battle. There are several possible reasons for Valens leaving Adrianople without the baggage train. The most obvious was that the baggage train would have slowed the army down too much, especially if the army was going to be marching over rough terrain rather than going by road. The next reason, and one I believe was Valens' main reason for leaving the baggage train behind, was that the Gothic camp must have been close enough to Adrianople to both march to and then return back the same day. The problem with the first reason is that why on earth would an army march to engage in battle without taking food, water and other essential supplies, including the spare weapons and armour, that the baggage would have been carrying? It just does not make any sense. But what if, despite Ammianus' claims, Valens did not intend fighting a battle at all? What if he intended doing exactly what Fritigern had suggested in the secret letter that was discussed in the previous chapter, i.e. Valens was marching to the Gothic encampment in a show of force in order to impress upon the Goths behind the wagons that it was in their best interest to enter into an agreement with the Romans. It was entirely possible that Valens was marching his army to Fritigern's camp in order to enter into negotiations with Fritigern, and then once the negotiations were completed taking refreshment with the now compliant Goths before returning back to

Adrianople before nightfall. There can be no other explanation why Valens, who, whilst not in the same league militarily as his brother Valentinian, and was an experienced and competent military commander, would march with practically his entire army in the blazing heat without taking its baggage train. Taking this evidence into account the only conclusion can be that Valens did not expect to fight a battle that day, something that may well have clouded his tactical judgement once the army had deployed.

Another clue to Valens' intentions was Ammianus' claim that the army had left the baggage and its packs guarded by several legions in their camp near to the walls of Adrianople, whilst the treasury and the imperial council were placed within the walls of the city itself. Valens obviously did not feel the need to place everything behind the walls of Adrianople, and felt secure enough to leave part of his army behind in the camp outside the walls. And the part of the army that was left behind may well have proved crucial to the battle itself had Valens really intended to fight on that day. If I am correct in believing that Valens' army contained ten legions then a 'suitable guard' would, I feel, be at the most four of those legions. It may well be that a similar number of auxiliary troops were also left behind in the camp. This would have meant that Valens in all probability marched towards the Goths with an army comprised of six legions, six auxiliary units and cavalry of various types. This would equate to Valens leaving Adrianople and marching to the Gothic encampment with approximately 18,000 infantry and possibly 3,000–6,000 cavalry.

Taking the size of the army into account then raised the question of how long the length of the column was as it marched towards the Gothic camp. Sources that give details of how a Roman marching column was formed are rare. From the information we do have is that the column size would be determined by the width of any road the troops would have been travelling on. The width of an average Roman road was approximately 18ft. If we presume there was a gap of 3ft between each infantry file, which just about allows six men to march abreast along the average road. If we say there were 1,000 infantry tasked with scouting at the head of the column, and a similar number protecting the rear of the column, that would have meant that there were 16,000 infantry remaining marching along the road. Each of the six files of infantry would have comprised of almost 2,666 men. If we say that the gap between each row of the file was 6ft then that would have meant that the infantry marching along the road would have been in a column approximately 16,000 feet long. This is just over three miles. We then have to add in the two scouting infantry groups, who were probably much more dispersed, so say add another mile to the infantry total. We also have to figure in the cavalry who also would have been travelling with the column. If we say there were 5,000 cavalry present, who were divided to the front, right flank, rear and in the column itself (as Ammianus implies the column was formed, see below), then we could say that there were 500 cavalry scouting in the front, 500 protecting the rear, 2,000 protecting the right flank and the remaining 2,000 imbedded in the column itself. If we say that a maximum of four cavalrymen could ride along the same road, and they needed a depth of 15ft, and they were divided 500 to the front of the column, 500 to the rear 2,000 to the right flank and the rest within the column itself, then we have an extra column depth of approximately 2 miles. If we add an extra mile for the cavalry who were scouting in front and those protecting the rear of the column this gives us a grand total for the length of the column of at least seven to eight miles. Increasing or decreasing the width of the column would of course have reduced or increased the depth, so if the column were eight men wide then we were probably looking at it being approximately 4 miles long, a four man wide column nearer 10 to 12 miles long. The implications of the length of the column will be discussed below.

Ammianus' text then continues:

So, after hastening a long distance over rough ground, whilst the hot day was advancing towards noon, finally at the eighth hour they saw the wagons of the enemy, which as a report of the scouts had declared, were arranged in the form of a perfect circle.

As I have stated above, the Romans must surely have known exactly where the wagon laager was because scouts would have kept it under constant observation. Also, the Gothic envoy that Fritigern had despatched the previous day must have been escorted by Roman troops to ensure that they were not attacked by mistake. This is a clear indication that the Goths cannot have been more than maximum of half a day's ride away, because the Gothic envoy and those that accompanied him were able to reach Adrianople, have a meeting with Valens and then return back to their encampment all within the same day.

According to Ammianus, Valens and his army marched 'a long distance over rough ground', Zosimus claimed that the army was also in 'complete disarray'.[3] Donnelly questions Rolfe's translation of Ammianus at this point, believing that the Latin text '*viarum spatiis conflagosis*' means nothing more than that the troops were quickly manoeuvring over rough terrain, not travelling a 'long distance over rough ground', something that I have come to agree with. It was of course possible that the army was in disarray when it left Adrianople and marched towards Fritigern's camp: it would have been unable to keep in a tight formation due to the nature of terrain it was travelling through, if it were indeed not travelling by road and instead travelling over rough ground. And this is another important point to note, why did Valens travel across the rough terrain? Could the army not have taken roads to reach the Goths? It may be that the roads from Adrianople did not offer a way of getting to the Goths quickly, or it could be that the roads the Roman army was taking took it across rough terrain, or the roads themselves were little more than trails?

Ammianus stated it was 'whilst the hot day was advancing towards noon' when the wagons of the Goths were sighted. And Rolfe's translation adds that it was 'at the eighth hour' when the Romans actually arrived at the Gothic wagons. The 'eighth hour' would be approximately 1.00 pm at that time of the year in the Roman method of time keeping. The Roman day was split into twelve daylight hours, the length of which varied depending on whether it was winter or summer. So, the army would have calculated the time in Summer Hours on 9 August. This would have meant that the army had been marching for at least six hours before sighting the Gothic camp, which I cannot believe because it would have meant that there was no chance for the army to march back to Adrianople before nightfall once it had reached the camp. Rolfe's translation has been called into question at this point; why mention noon and then the 'eighth hour' as being when the Gothic camp was seen? I am inclined to believe that the Gothic camp was actually seen by the Roman scouts at a distance of 8 miles into the march, as Blockley has suggested. The scouts may have been a mile or so ahead of the column, and the wagons may have been several miles further in the distance, giving the distance of the wagons from Adrianople at twelve miles. Most modern commentators place the Gothic camp at between eight and fifteen miles from Adrianople. Only one ancient account gives an actual distance for the Gothic camp, the 'Consularia Constantiopolitana' which states that it was at a distance of 'the twelfth milestone' (an indication the Gothic encampment was near a road?). Ammianus may have indicated in Book XXXI, 12, 3 that the Goths were fifteen miles from Adrianople and heading south-east towards Nike, but that was when Valens was already en route to Adrianople from Melanthias, and the Goths must have moved on several miles before Valens arrived and pitched his camp outside the walls of Adrianople. A Roman mile was approximately 1,617 yards, which would make the distance to the twelfth milestone approximately eleven modern International Miles. I am happy to go with the Gothic camp being a maximum of twelve miles away from Adrianople as being the middle ground between the lowest and highest figures given for the location of the battlefield. This would have been an easy distance for the Gothic envoys mentioned in the previous chapter to have travelled to Adrianople and back to their camp within a single day if on horseback, or even by foot if travelling by road. It should also have been a very easy distance to cover by a Roman army in a matter of hours under normal circumstances. As stated in Chapter Nine, Vegetius stated that a Roman army could travel twenty miles in five Summer Hours, and other sources give comparable rates of travel.[4] Whether this was by road or not is a good question, as undoubtedly travelling by road was going to be much quicker than travelling over rough ground, especially if taking along a baggage train. But as we know, Valens did not take the baggage train along with the army, so the rate of march must have been quicker even if they were travelling over broken terrain. Taking this into account, if the Gothic camp was at a distance of eight to twelve miles from Adrianople, and was seen by the Roman scouts at a distance of eight miles at noon, this would have meant that Valens' army was travelling at a speed of only approximately 1.33/1.5 miles an hour instead of the average of 4 miles an hour when it sighted the wagons, a very slow rate of march indeed. Either the ground Valens was travelling over was extremely rough, or he and his army were travelling extremely slowly. Or, Valens was travelling by a route that was longer but which would have been from a direction the Goths were not expecting. Logic would suggest the most direct route was taken as Valens was stated by most accounts as wanting to get to the Gothic camp as quickly as possible. But if this were true then how does this again explain the fact that the Goths the following day reached Adrianople in less than four hours, yet Valens took at least seven hours to reach those same wagons? There are several possible explanations for this. The first one, and completely overlooked by other commentators of the battle, is that Valens' army was marching in a column at least eight miles long. The head of the column would have arrived at the Gothic encampment at least three, perhaps three and a half hours after leaving Adrianople, if the column was travelling at a speed of between 2 to 4 miles per hour. It would have started to form up into the usual Roman battle formation (see below and also Chapter Fifteen) and this would have taken between three and four hours because that would have been the length of time it would have taken for the rear of the column to have reached the wagons. This fits the evidence, it took seven hours for the entire Roman army to reach the wagons and then deploy into battle formation, it did not take seven hours just to travel to the encampment, and then the troops deployed in to the battle formation.

The other possible reason for the delay in reaching the wagons, and which would fit in with Ammianus' account, was that Valens took a longer route, one which he considered was the best to take to ensure the Goths were not going to be aware of his arrival. If this is so then it's my view that this longer route was achieved by the army following the course of the Tonzos River north before turning north-east. This will be fully explored below.

Although the army may initially have not travelled by road, later in Ammianus' text there is an indication that the army undertook the last stage of their journey by road, which may have speeded up the travel somewhat, and may have led to a doubling in the rate of the marching armies' speed. This could explain why the last hour of the journey to the wagons only took an hour, which brought the rate of march back up to 4 miles an hour, the usual rate by road.

Ammianus stated that the Roman scouts reported that when the wagons were sighted they were arranged in a 'perfect circle'.[5] Some, such as Donnelly and McDowell, have chosen to dispute this, stating that the estimated number of 5,000 Gothic wagons that may have been present, taking into account the minimum number of Gothic warriors and their families etc would have taken up a vast area if arranged in a circle. Donnelly believes instead that the wagons were arranged in a semi-circle forming a barrier, whilst McDowell has them in lines, like a barricade. I believe both are wrong. I see no issue with the wagons forming a circle, the pioneers travelling across the 'boundless wastes' of America formed their wagons in protective circles, it appears the natural thing to do. Whilst Donnelly calculated that the wagon circle would have had to have been at least 1,700m or 5,600 ft in circumference if 5,000 wagons were present, this is only a diameter of 1,800 ft or 540m. This is based on a hollow circle made up of just one ring of wagons. However, as shown in diagrams 2–5 the wagons could have been formed up in either spiral-like formation or of concentric circles to cut down on the diameter, or even several such circles could have been formed, one next to the other.

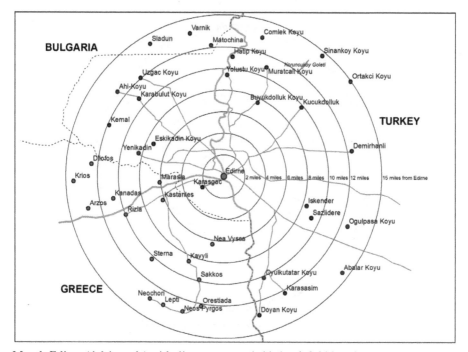

Map 1: Edirne (Adrianople) with distances to probable battlefield locations.

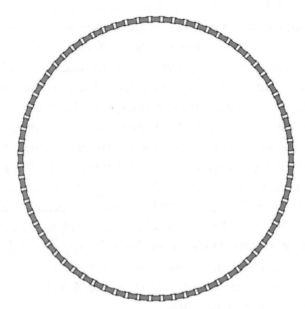

Diagram 1: Gothic wagon laager in single ring.

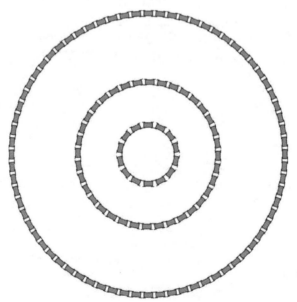

Diagram 2: Gothic wagon laager in concentric rings.

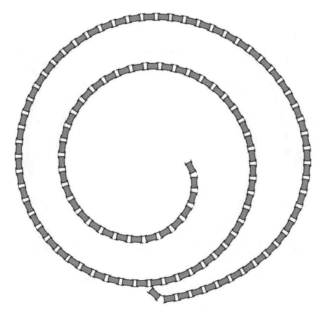

Diagram 3: Gothic wagon laager in spiral formation

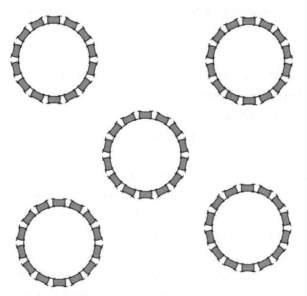

Diagram 4: Gothic wagon laager in group formation

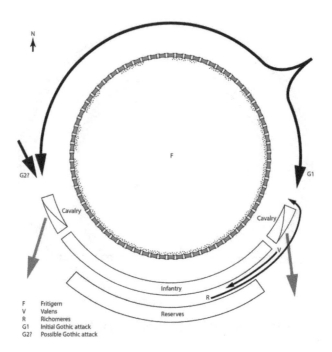

Diagram 5: Roman deployment in front of Goth wagons with direction of Gothic cavalry attacks displayed

Where the Gothic wagons in relation to Adrianople were is unfortunately unknown. However see Chapter Fourteen where I discuss possible locations for the site of the battlefield.

Going back to the text of Ammianus he stated-

And while the barbarian soldiers, according to their custom, uttered savage and dismal howls, the Roman leaders ('*duces*') so drew up their line of battle that the cavalry on the right wing were first pushed forward, whilst the greater part of the infantry waited in reserve. But the left wing of the horsemen (which was formed with the greatest difficulty, since very many of them were still scattered along the roads) was hastening to the spot at swift pace, and whilst that same wing was being extended, still without interruption, the barbarians were terrified by the awful din, the hiss of whirring arrows and the menacing clash of shields ...

As discussed above, Valens' army was marching in a column, probably with mounted scouts at the front and rear, with outriders to the flanks. The cavalry would normally be at the head of the column behind the scouts and also riding by either side of the column, protecting the flanks of the infantry and the baggage train. The infantry would have followed behind, then the baggage train, and finally the 'light infantry', along with the rest of the cavalry, protecting the rear of the column. This is advocated by Vegetius and also in Arrian's 'Array against the Alans'.[6] It is also easier to deploy in the 'typical' Roman battle formation when marching in this manner, i.e. with cavalry on the wings and infantry forming in the centre. This would have been achieved by the cavalry on the right flank moving forward and to the right to form the right wing of the army, the infantry then moving forward and to the right to then start forming the centre, with the cavalry on the column's left flank moving forward and to the left to create the left wing, the light troops coming forward to screen the deployment and prevent the deployment being disrupted by the enemy. However, from the text it appears that the cavalry that was supposed to form the left wing was actually imbedded with the infantry in the main column and not on the flank as would normally have been the case – 'But the left wing of the horsemen, (which was formed with the greatest difficulty, since very many of them were still scattered along the roads) was hastening to the spot at a swift pace.' From this we note several points, the first and most important, and often overlooked by others, was that the army was now travelling by 'roads' at this juncture. This may have a bearing on where to look for the battle site for archaeologists for they can now narrow the site down to an area that had roads at a distance of 8 to 12 miles from Adrianople at that date. The column does not appear to have marched with the cavalry protecting the left flank, as Ammianus notes it was travelling along the roads, presumably with the rest of the infantry in the column. One possible reason for this was that there was no need for the cavalry to be covering the left flank as the left flank was being protected by something else, perhaps a natural feature. What natural feature could protect the flank of a marching army from attack? A steep ridge or rugged mountains might be able to, there are many such features in that region (Google Earth is a very good resource and using it shows exactly what the terrain looks like around Edirne today). The most logical natural defence near Adrianople would have been the Tonzos River known in Roman times as the Hebrus. The Tonzos River lies to the west of modern Edirne (Adrianople) and it flows north and then north-west into Bulgaria. Any Goths in the area would have been unable to mount an attack across the river without them being in the full view of any Roman army travelling along its east bank, and those troops would have had ample time to form up and repulse any such attack before the Goths could cross over. If Valens was not taking a route directly towards the Goths then the evidence points to the army travelling along the east bank of the Tonzos before taking a road north-east towards the battlefield because that would be the most plausible explanation for the left wing cavalry being in the column with the infantry. Travelling along the river would also have allowed the troops to take water directly from it.

As noted above, the 'Roman leaders', presumably Valens, Richomeres, Sebastianus, Victor and Trajanus, gave orders for the army to deploy in the typical Roman battle formation once the wagons had been sighted (see Chapter Fifteen). This deployment appears to have been completed long before the arrival of the Gothic cavalry. The clue to this is the next part of the text of Ammianus where he tells us 'And while that same wing was being extended, still without interruption, the barbarians were terrified by the awful din, the hiss of whirring arrows and the menacing clash of shields'. The Goths would have been alerted to the presence of the Roman army long before they saw any actual troops. This would have been due to the clouds of dust rising above the Roman column; this dust cloud would have been seen for miles on that clear summer's day. One can only imagine the scene within the Gothic encampment at that point. The Gothic warriors would have been filled with a mixture of both dread and grim determination, demanding Fritigern and the other chieftain to tell them what to do. Their families would no doubt have been filled with a mixture of panic and fear at the approach of the Romans. Once the Roman army was actually seen to be approaching along the road, and then observed to be deploying before the wagons, it's no wonder the Goths started raising their war cries and appealing to their God and ancestors for protection from what they no doubt believed was the battle to come. The Goths do not appear to have made any effort at this point to interrupt the Roman army from deploying in battle formation. In fact the Romans appear to have been able to form their left wing under the protection of bow fire, probably from both bow-armed cavalry attached to the cavalry forming the left wing as well as bow- armed infantry skirmishers. Whilst the left wing was deploying, the Roman infantry began making a lot of noise by clashing their weapons against their shields. This was no doubt to deter the Goths from leaving the wagons.[7] Once the army had fully deployed the formation at this point may well have resembled a semi-circle, mirroring the section of the Gothic wagon laager the army was facing. This would have led to the Roman army curving around the wagons with both cavalry wings forming the extremities of this semicircular formation with the infantry in the centre of the formation (see diagram 5). This formation would have exposed the flanks and rear of the Roman cavalry to any Goths not directly approaching from the wagons and may explain the actions of the Roman cavalry once battle was joined. The deployment was in all probability completed between 1.00 pm and 3.00 pm at the latest, depending on whether Valens took the direct route or the longer one following the Tonzos River.

It is useful at this point to try and speculate as to the general direction the Roman army was facing when it was deployed, because it may indicate the direction where the Gothic cavalry came from. If the army was marching in a north-easterly direction when the Gothic wagons were sighted then it is not too presumptuous to assume that the army deployed with the centre of the army facing north or north-east. This would have meant that the sun would have either have been behind or to the right side of where the army was facing the wagons. This was a tactically sound deployment advocated in a number of Roman military manuals: having the sun behind you, and the enemy facing into the sun, places the enemy at a distinct disadvantage, especially when it comes to employing missile fire as the sun would have dazzled those looking in its direction.

At this point in the text of Ammianus he lays the ground for the suspicion that the Goths are up to no good, that they are stalling for time and that what was to happen was all part of some nefarious Gothic plan. He wrote:

> … and since a part of their forces under Alatheus and Saphrax was far away and, though sent for, had not yet returned, they sent envoys to beg for peace. The emperor scorned these because of their low origin,

demanding for the execution of a lasting treaty that suitable chieftains be sent; meanwhile the enemy purposely delayed, in order that during the pretended truce their cavalry might return, who, they hoped, would soon make their appearance; also that our soldiers might be exposed to the fiery summer heat and exhausted by their dry throats, whilst the broad plains gleamed with fires, which the enemy were feeding with wood and dry fuel, for this same purpose. To that evil was added another deadly one, namely, that men and beasts were tormented by severe hunger.

Some points need examining in this statement. Firstly, Ammianus stated that the Gothic cavalry were 'far away' without stating where they were. It's likely that the Gothic cavalry were out foraging for supplies. They must have been a fair distance away because they did not arrive until a few hours after the Roman army's deployment. The envoys sent by Fritigern sound similar to the ones sent the previous evening, although why Fritigern had sent envoys whose lowly stature would not have been accepted is a mystery. Unless of course Fritigern was once again sending his Christian envoy, with the attendant 'humble folk' as further example that as a fellow Christian his intentions were honourable? There is an interesting thought here: were the Goths also hoping that Valens had the same physical disposition and temper of his brother Valentinian, would Valens fly into a fit of rage and thus trigger a stroke with fatal consequences?

As I noted above, it does not take much imagination to visualize the scene behind the Gothic wagons. The Gothic warriors and their families, seeing the Roman army deploying before their encampment, were no doubt beseeching Fritigern and the other Gothic nobles to enter into negotiations to prevent an assault and the ensuing slaughter. Up to this point Valens at least was following the plan as suggested by Fritigern, namely to show the rest of the Goths his army in full battle array and ready to fight.

The suspicion that the Goths were delaying things for as long as possible to allow the return of their cavalry is raised when Ammianus describes how the Roman troops were beginning to suffer the effects of not only the fierce heat of the summer sun, but they were also suffering from smoke inhalation from the grass fires set by the Goths and also from lack of food and water. I believe that the fires were set initially as a way of alerting the Gothic cavalry to the presence of the Roman army, or they may have lit as a pre-planned signal for the cavalry to return. The fires would have sent up plumes of smoke that would have alerted the foraging Gothic cavalry that they needed to return. The smoke plumes would also have helped mask the dust cloud raised by the Gothic cavalry as they headed towards the wagons. As stated above, the Goths behind the wagons would have seen the cloud of dust raised by the Romans on their march towards the Gothic encampment long before the Romans actually came into sight. They must have been aware that the Romans would in turn see the dust cloud raised by their returning cavalry. A smoke screen would do the job nicely of concealing the approach of their cavalry; and that is why the Romans were caught totally unaware of their arrival. It was an unintended, but useful side effect to have that smoke then blow into the faces of the Romans facing the wagons! At this stage it also appears Fritigern was sticking to his part of the deal according to Ammianus:

> Meanwhile, Fritigern, shrewd to foresee the future and fearing the uncertainty of war, on his own initiative sent one of his common soldiers as a herald, requesting picked men of noble rank be sent to him at once as hostages and saying that he himself would fearlessly meet the threats of his soldiers and do what was necessary.

Fritigern was in an awkward position, his troops were no doubt demanding action and without his cavalry to hand, any hostile action against the Romans was potentially disastrous, so he was forced to do 'what was necessary' and commence negotiations. This could well be an allusion to the contents of the letter received by Valens from Fritigern the day before at Adrianople where Fritigern had suggested Valens 'show them (the Goths) near at hand his army ready for battle, and through the fear aroused by the imperial name check their destructive eagerness for war'. There is no reason to suspect any treachery at this point on Fritigern's behalf. Valens may have believed his army outnumbered the Goths behind the wagons by a factor of at least two to one, and he could have ordered an attack at any moment, with a very real chance of inflicting a crushing defeat upon the Goths. It is at this point that in all probability the disaster of the Battle of Adrianople actually took place. Valens had a golden opportunity to attack the Goths whilst they were at a severe disadvantage. The Goths were penned up behind their wagons and they still did not have any cavalry to provide them with additional support. I doubt very much that had the Roman army attacked the Goths at this stage then the Gothic cavalry arriving several hours later would have saved the day. More likely the returning Gothic cavalry would have arrived just in time to see a mass slaughter of their kinsmen within the Gothic encampment. That is if in fact they would have returned at all, because any deserters or survivors from the Gothic encampment would have naturally have fled toward the direction they knew their cavalry was coming from, and once informed of the disaster at the wagons those cavalry would have naturally sought safety in flight themselves.

Was Fritigern actually making good on his word and actually wanting to enter into treaty arrangements? Fritigern probably had no idea of how long it would take for the Gothic cavalry to return and he was no doubt acutely aware that should Valens order an immediate attack he and the rest of the Goths behind the wagons faced almost certain defeat and destruction. If Valens was prepared to meet most of Fritigern's demands then a treaty could have been hammered out that would have been advantageous for both sides. The Goths would have a new homeland whilst Valens would have a new source of recruits for his delayed invasion of Sassanid Persia. There is absolutely nothing to indicate Fritigern was deliberately delaying to allow the return of the Gothic cavalry. In fact it's likely Fritigern had no idea that the cavalry would arrive at all. No, it's more the case that it was better for Ammianus and others to claim it was Gothic duplicity that led to the Roman defeat rather than admitting that it was a case of extremely bad timing on the Gothic cavalry's behalf, coupled with Valens not ordering an immediate attack that led to the Roman defeat at Adrianople.

It is entirely possible that at this point of the engagement Valens had sent messengers to the camp outside of Adrianople for the troops stationed there to come to the army's aid. He could even have attempted to summon them beforehand if we accept that Valens was himself being duplicitous, using the negotiations as a way of giving time for the potential reinforcements to arrive. Whatever the case was, negotiations were eagerly entered into by both sides.

The proposal of the dreaded leader was welcome and approved, and the tribune Aequitius, then marshal of the court, and a relative of Valens, with the general consent was chosen to go speedily as a surety. When he objected, on the ground that he had once been captured by the enemy but had escaped from Dibaltum, and therefore feared their unreasonable anger, Richomeres voluntarily offered his own services and gladly promised to go, thinking this also to be a fine act and worthy of a brave man. And soon he was on his way (bringing) proofs of his rank and birth.

Valens and his council were no doubt eager to enter into negotiations at this point as reports must have reached him that his men were suffering from the effects of both lack of food, water, and from the extreme heat of the day. Valens needed to get the treaty signed and take the army back to Adrianople before nightfall. If the army had deployed by between 1.00 pm and 2.00 pm then the negotiations between Valens and Fritigern probably commenced after the army deployed. The negotiations would have taken at least an hour, probably two, so if Valens did indeed return to Adrianople he would have had to leave the Gothic encampment by 5.00 pm at the very latest to prevent the entire column having to march in the darkness.

It was probably of great relief to have Fritigern asking for hostages to be exchanged as that indicated a serious gesture on his behalf, and there would be no recourse to fighting a battle after all. Again, Valens had no reason to doubt Fritigern, up to this point both of them appear to still be sticking to the plan outlined in the secret letter sent the previous day. We do not know how long the debate between Valens and his inner council took, not too long one would have thought and it must have been a shock to Valens when Aequitius declined the 'honour' of being a hostage, citing he had recently been a captive of the Goths but managed to escape and feared Gothic retribution.[8] It must have astonished all those present at the debate when at this point Richomeres volunteered to go in Aequitius' place. Richomeres was one of the most reputable and ablest commanders in Valens' army, one whose generalship would surely have been better employed outside of the Gothic camp rather than in it! This was a massive blunder on Valens' behalf and perhaps tells us something about Valens' state of mind at that point.

Valens surely could not have been expecting a Gothic attack or he would have never allowed Richomeres to offer his services as a hostage. Whatever the case was, Richomeres set off towards the Gothic wagons with 'proofs of his rank and birth'. He never arrived. At this very moment Bellona sounded her mournful horn and the Battle of Adrianople began.

Before proceeding to the discussion of the battle itself, it is at this point that the positions on the battlefield of Valens and his commanders become important. Publius Flavius Vegetius Renatus, better known as Vegetius, wrote a work, *Epitoma Rei Militaris*, better known as the *Epitome of Military Science*, sometime between AD 385 and AD 450. It was not an entirely original work; Vegetius used surviving military manuals and treatises by Celcus, Cato, Frontinus and Paternus amongst others to put together his *Epitome*, using what he believed to be the best bits from them all. It is clear from the text of the *Epitome* that it is a mixture of both ancient and contemporary practice, using as he does descriptions of current military arms, i.e. the term *Spiculum* for the standard Roman spear being just one example. *Book III: Field Strategy and Tactics*, Chapter 18 details, 'In what position the commander-in-chief, the second- and third-in-command should stand.' This chapter indicated that if Valens was commanding the army he should have been located on the right hand side of the main infantry force between the juncture of the infantry and the right flank cavalry. Richomeres, as the second-in-command should have been with the infantry in the centre facing the wagon laager, or if he was actually taking command of the army, then he would have been positioned between the infantry and cavalry on the right. Sebastianus, as third-in-command, would have been positioned on the left flank, between the infantry and the left flank cavalry. When Richomeres elected to go to the Gothic camp then Sebastianus would have taken his position in the centre with the infantry. It was highly unlikely Richomeres would have allowed the infantry lines to be broken up in order to allow him and his escorting cavalry through. Richomeres would have had to have taken a route towards the Gothic encampment going around the back of the infantry towards either the left or right hand side of either flanks' cavalry then gone around those flanking cavalry to then head towards the wagons. I believe Richomeres headed towards the right side of the flanking Roman cavalry for reasons I will give below.

As Richomeres was heading towards the Gothic wagons disaster stuck.

As he was on his way to the enemy's rampart, the archers (*Sagittarii*) and the targeteers (*Scutarii*), then under the command of one Bacurius of Hiberia and Cassio, had rushed forward too eagerly in hot attack, and were already engaged with their adversaries; and as their charge had been untimely, their retreat was cowardly; and thus they gave an unfavourable omen to the beginning of the battle.

What had happened? The *Sagittarii* and the *Scutarii* were most likely the *Scola Scutariorum Prima* and the *Scola Scutariorum Sagittariorum*, two cavalry guard units who I believe were tasked with escorting Richomeres over to the Gothic encampment. There is no clue from the text of Ammianus or any other of the surviving histories who the *Sagitarii* and the *Scutarii* were attacking. Most historians feel it was the returning cavalry of Alatheus and Saphrax, although this is not implied by Ammianus. He appears instead to imply that the attack of Bacurius and Cassio was already underway when the Gothic cavalry made its appearance. It may well be the case that Fritigern had tasked some of his Goths to greet Richomeres and his escort, and that the units under the command of Bacurius and Cassio, for whatever reason, then attacked these Goths and then the cavalry under Bacurius and Cassio were then unceremoniously beaten off. I agree it's not unreasonable to suggest that it was in fact the leading elements of the returning Gothic cavalry Bacurius and Cassio tangled with, especially if it was the case that Richomeres was making his way to the Gothic camp by going around the right flank of the Roman army.

Ammianus continued:

This unseasonable proceeding not only thwarted the prompt action of Richomeres, who was not allowed to go at all, but also the Gothic cavalry, returning with Alatheus and Saphrax, combined with a band of Halani (Alans), dashed out as a thunderbolt does near high mountains, and threw into confusion all those whom they could find in the way of their swift onslaught, and quickly slew them.

The flight of the *Sagittarii* and the *Scutarii* caused the right wing cavalry to falter and flee from the battlefield once they saw the *Scutarii* and *Sagittarii* hotly pursued by the Gothic cavalry.[9] The brittleness of Roman cavalry units is shown within the text of Ammianus, even the lauded Catafractarii/ Clibanarii were not immune to being routed, taking the rest of the cavalry with them, as happened at Argentoratum AD 357.[10]

So, from which direction on the battlefield had the Gothic cavalry appeared? This is another question that has long vexed historians. This would have depended on what direction the centre of the Roman army was facing towards the Gothic wagons. If the Romans had been marching northwards towards the Gothic camp then the conclusion would be that the centre of the Roman army would have been facing north, but if it were then curved inwards to follow the curve of the Goth wagons then the left wing would have been facing north-easterly and the right wing facing north-westerly. However, we have no idea of what direction the Roman army was facing, it could as easily have been facing east or west or points in between. However see my earlier comments in this chapter for my views on the direction the Romans were facing, and the reasons why. What we can say with some confidence is that the Roman army could not have been facing southwards as this would have meant the Romans having to march around the camp before deploying and Ammianus tells us that the Romans began deploying almost straight after they sighted the Gothic wagons. Also Ammianus states that the sun was over the heads of the Romans, indicating they were not facing into the sun. I am inclined to believe that the Romans were deployed facing in some northward facing direction, keeping the sun out of their eyes but with the sun beating down directly upon their backs. This only slightly helps us to fix the direction of the appearance of the Gothic cavalry. For one thing, we can almost certainly eliminate the Gothic horse appearing in the rear of the Romans as this would have meant that they would have come from the same direction of the Roman route of march, and it's highly unlikely that the Goths would have sent messengers out to summon the Gothic cavalry if they had to pass by the Romans heading in their direction! So are there any clues as to the initial direction that the Gothic cavalry hit the Roman lines? Well, possibly. If the Gothic cavalry were away foraging for supplies, it was probably the case that these supplies were more likely to be found near to bodies of water, because crops need water in order to grow. If McDowell (2001) is right and the battlefield was located near to Muratcali, then it's likely the Gothic Cavalry would have been foraging near to the Tonzos River to the west. There is a problem with this suggestion in that the Tonzos River is only an hour's fast ride away at most from Muratcali, and the cavalry coming from that direction would have initially attacked the Roman left flank, and I believe the Goths initially attacked the right flank. There is of course the possibility that the Gothic cavalry were not out in one group, they may have been split into a number of groups and these groups returned at the battlefield at different times, which would have explained why the Roman left flank infantry were able to assault the wagons before the Gothic cavalry arrived on that flank and drove off the Roman cavalry. However, if Runkel (1904) is right and the battle was near to Demirhanli, then it's likely the Gothic cavalry would have been coming from the east as there is a large source of water at Habiller Sulama Goleti, or even northeast at Geckinli Goleti; this would also have meant that farms would have been located near to these water sources where food and fodder could have been plundered. This last source of water could also have been used if the Goths were camped in the area between Korucu, Sinankoy and Ortakci. They could also have obtained water from a lake near Taslimusellim in the north-east. So, Korucu and Sinankov would have required the Gothic horse to have approached the Romans from the north-east, from Ortakci from the north-east or from almost due east. Of course if it was just water that the cavalry were sent to collect then they could have taken the water from any local stream, but why then were they described as being 'far away', which would be the case if they were foraging around the Tonzos River or around the other bodies of water I have mentioned. I am of course fully aware of my previous caveat in that earthquakes in this region may have obliterated the original water sources and the large bodies of water may have not existed in AD 378 that I described above. However, if they did exist, as does the Tonzos now, then we have three choices from where the Gothic cavalry came from. They either came from the west/north-west (Muratcali), north/north-east (Korucu, Sinankov, Demirhanli and Ortakci), or east (Ortakci and Demirhanli). There is also fourth possibility, which is a more speculative one. Were the Gothic cavalry that attacked the Romans not the ones that were out foraging for supplies, but instead were those despatched by Fritigern to scout the way to Constantinople and who had arrived unexpectedly? If they were then they would have been coming from either the north-east or from an easterly direction. If however they were coming from the Tonzos River, this would have meant them striking the Roman lines from a westerly direction, which seems unlikely as all the evidence points to an attack on the right flank.

Having established that the Gothic cavalry could have arrived in one of three directions, possibly of course from more than one direction at once, can we say which of these three directions is more likely? If I am right in my argument that Richomeres moved around the right flank with his escort and his escort then engaged in combat with the Goths, then the Gothic cavalry must have come from the north-east. See further arguments on this point below.

The Gothic cavalry's arrival initiated a general engagement, the Gothic cavalry then charging into the Roman infantry line after the Roman right wing cavalry routed. Chaos and confusion reigned within the Roman lines.

Ammianus described it graphically:

On every side armour and weapons clashed, and Bellona, raging with more than usual madness for the destruction of the Romans, blew her lamentable war-trumpets; our soldiers who were giving way rallied, exchanging many encouraging shouts, but the battle, spreading like flames, filled their hearts with terror, as numbers of them were pierced by strokes of whirling spears and arrows. Then the lines dashed together like beaked ships, pushing each other back and forth in turn, and tossed about by alternate movements, like waves at sea.

Now, we have to understand that as Ammianus was not at the battle in person he could not have really known what happened. He could however use his previous military experience as a Tribune in the Roman army, fighting in campaigns both in the West and East, to give an insight to what it must have been like for the troops at that battle. He also must have relied on both personal accounts from survivors of the battle, and other histories written after the battle itself, and now sadly lost, for his information. Much of what he said about the battle may well have more than a touch of artistic licence about it, he was after all telling a story, but there must be a great deal of truth mixed in with the flavour of the story.

From the above we can see that the arrival of the Gothic cavalry led to a general engagement, with what appears some Gothic infantry being present outside of the wagons also attacking the Roman lines. This is evidenced by the phrase 'Then the lines dashed together like beaked ships, pushing each other back and forth in turn.' This sounds more like an infantry clash where opposing men push against the enemies' shields to try and overwhelm them rather than a mass of cavalry trying to break through the Roman lines. 'Beaked ships' could be a reference to infantry on both sides being in '*cuneus*' or 'wedge' shaped formations, which both the Romans and other Germanic enemies had been noted by Ammianus as using in a number of battles in his history. There is no indication who is throwing the spears or firing the arrows, probably a mixture of both Gothic infantry and their horsemen. The Roman line appears to have stabilized and there is no indication that things will go from bad to worse very rapidly. However, it was at this point that it appears the Roman cavalry, what remained of it on the battlefield at least, deserted the infantry and left them to certain doom.

And because the left wing, which had made its way as far as the very wagons, and would have gone farther if it had had any support, being deserted by the rest of the cavalry, was hard pressed by the enemy's numbers, it was crushed, and over-whelmed, as if by the downfall of a mighty rampart.

Sozomen stated 'His (Valens') cavalry was dispersed, his infantry compelled to retreat.'

Or as Socrates put it '… the cavalry revolted and refused to engage, the infantry were surrounded by the barbarians'.

Orosius echoed these two when he stated 'As soon as the squadrons of Roman cavalry were thrown into confusion by the sudden attack of the Goths, they left the companies of infantrymen without protection.'

Now, back to a point I made earlier about which direction the attacking Gothic cavalry had come from. If the Gothic cavalry had appeared towards the Roman right flank this would account for the fact that the Roman left wing had time to actually move up to and assault the defenders behind the Gothic wagons. It would also account for the fact that there appears to have been a combined attack from both the Gothic cavalry and Gothic infantry on the right side of the Roman army, which does not appear to have happened on the Roman left flank because if it had then Ammianus would surely have mentioned that the Romans on the left had engaged and beaten the Goths back towards the protection of the wagons. One can imagine the scene where the Goths in the wagon laager, observing the Gothic cavalry appearing and attacking the Roman right wing cavalry and driving it away, openly left the wagon laager and joined in the assault on the Roman infantry nearest that flank. The Roman left wing, and possibly the Goths behind the wagons facing them, may have been blissfully unaware of events on the Roman right until the Roman cavalry on the left suddenly deserted. And why would the Roman cavalry on the left suddenly desert if the infantry they were supporting were on the threshold of actually storming the wagons? There can only be one explanation: more Gothic cavalry appeared out of the blue on the Roman left, causing the Roman cavalry to panic and flee the battlefield. Now, either these Goths were new arrivals, having come from a different direction and taken a bit longer to reach the battlefield, or, and more likely, they were part of the main Gothic cavalry group who had made their way around the back of the wagon laager, where no Roman forces were present to oppose them, and then suddenly appeared right on top of the Roman cavalry who were totally unaware of their presence, concentrating as they were on assisting the infantry who were attacking the Gothic defenders behind the wagons. It's no wonder then that the Roman cavalry on the left reeled back and then fled under this unforeseen attack, imitating as they did so their fellows on the right flank. So, it appears to me highly likely that the Gothic cavalry appeared on the Roman right flank and that part of it swept around the back of the wagon laager to chase away the Roman cavalry on the left flank. And it may not have been a very large number of Gothic cavalry required to do this either, even fifty cavalrymen appearing as if out of nowhere would seem like ten times their number to those who were not expecting their presence. It's almost certain that at this point there were no Roman cavalry remaining on the battlefield, none had been placed in reserve, the reserves had been all infantry according to Ammianus. The battle now moved rapidly towards the decisive end game:

The foot-soldiers thus stood unprotected, and their companies (*manipulis*) were so crowded together that hardly anyone could pull out his sword or draw back his arm. Because of clouds of dust the heavens could no longer be seen, and echoed with frightful cries. Hence the arrows whirling death from every side always found their mark with fatal effect, since they could not be seen beforehand nor guarded against. But when the barbarians, pouring forth in huge hordes, trampled down horse and man, and in the press of ranks no room for retreat could be gained anywhere, and the increased crowding left no opportunity for escape, our soldiers also, showing extreme contempt of falling in the fight, received their death-blows, yet struck down their assailants; and on both sides the strokes of axes split helmet and breastplate. Here one might see a barbarian filled with lofty courage, his cheeks contracted in a hiss, hamstrung or with right hand severed, or pierced through the side, on the very verge of death threateningly casting about his fierce glance; and by the fall of the combatants on both sides the plains were covered with the bodies of the slain strewn over the ground, while the groans of the dying and of those who had suffered deep wounds caused immense fear when they were heard. In this great tumult and confusion the infantry, exhausted by their efforts and the danger, when in turn strength and mind for planning anything were lacking, their lances (*hastarum*) for the most part broken by constant clashing, content to fight with drawn swords, plunged into the dense masses of the foe, regardless of their lives, seeing all around that every loophole of escape was lost. The ground covered with streams of blood whirled their slippery foothold from under them, so they could only strain every nerve to sell their lives dearly; and they opposed the onrushing foe with such great resolution that some fell by the weapons of their own comrades. Finally, when the whole scene was discoloured with the hue of dark blood, and wherever men turned their eyes heaps of slain met them, they trod upon the bodies of the dead without mercy. Now the sun had risen higher, and when it had finished its course through Leo, and was passing into the house of the heavenly Virgo, and scorched the Romans, who were more and more exhausted by hunger and worn out by thirst, as well as distressed by the heavy burden of their armour.

Finally our line was broken by the onrushing weight of the barbarians, and since that was the only resort in their last extremity, they took to their heels in disorder as best they could.

Ammianus described here how the infantry 'stood unprotected' due to the flight of the remaining Roman cavalry and that they were 'so crowded together that hardly anyone could pull out his sword or draw back his arm'. This graphically illustrated that both flanks of the Roman army were being compressed at this point by Gothic troops attacking them from the left and right flanks. Gothic infantry left the wagon laager, in 'huge hordes', any fear of the Romans now vanished, and the Goths scented victory. This caused there to be a compressed, confused mass of men and horses, both Roman and Goth, all of which became trampled in the press. No retreat could be found for the Romans caught up in this confused melee. Of course, Ammianus is putting a bit of a spin on the Roman courage and determination in the face of defeat; it's not hard to see men surrounded on all sides fighting for their very lives not needing any sort of contempt for their own death! It's interesting here to note that at least some of the Romans appear to be armed with axes, which is not too surprising. The troops may have been issued with axes in case they were expected to assault the wagons as they would have needed a weapon able to cut through the wood of the wagons, and any barricades strung between the intervals of the wagons. The *Notitia Dignitatum*, an official record of the location of late Roman units and officials dating to around the AD '390s' to the '420s' shows a number of *fabracae* (factories) that produced axes of various types, so axes were not unknown to the late Roman army. The above statement also appears to show that the axes were strong enough to cut through both 'helmet and breastplate', or – as a more correct translation of '*loricae*' would be – 'body armour'.

Ammianus dramatically described how bravely the Goth warriors fought, how the battlefield became strewn with the bodies of the dead and dying, how the Roman spears became 'broken by constant clashing' and the infantry then having to rely solely on their drawn swords, and how the Roman infantry, surrounded on all sides, exhausted and with their strength failing, 'plunged into the dense masses of the foe, regardless of their lives, seeing all around that every loophole of escape was lost'. It is interesting that the Roman infantry appear to have retained their spears instead of throwing them into the Gothic mass as they may have been expected to do in previous times when they were armed with the *pilum*, despite Vegetius implying that *spiculum* had the same armour penetration ability of the *pilum* it appeared to have replaced. This gives some weight to the idea that Late Roman infantry at this date could fight in a foulkion type formation, a shield wall, relying mostly on their spear for hand to hand combat rather than the sword.[11] It may also be the case that as the Romans were fighting a mixture of both Gothic cavalry and infantry at this point so that retaining the spear to fend off the cavalry was a better tactic than throwing the spear on first contact. Whatever the case was, the Romans were still fighting hard at this point of the narrative, even when they were totally surrounded and no visible means of escape presented itself. However, this would not last long. The ground became soaked in blood and both sides were forced to trample over the bodies of the dead and dying. The sun was now beginning to head towards the horizon and the Romans began to suffer from exhaustion caused by 'hunger and worn out by thirst', as well as being 'distressed by the heavy burden of their armour'. At this critical moment disaster struck; as Ammianus put it: 'Finally our line was broken by the onrushing weight of the barbarians, and since that was the only resort in their last extremity, they took to their heels in disorder as best they could.' Without any visible support close to hand, it's not hard to see why the infantry took flight. The battle entered its end phase.

Whilst all this was happening, where was Valens? As stated earlier Valens, as commander-in-chief, should have been '...between the infantry and cavalry on the right flank. This is the position from which the whole line is commanded, and from which there is direct and unobstructed forward movement. He stands between the two arms so as to direct with his advice and exhort by his authority both cavalry and infantry to battle. It is his task to use his cavalry reserves with light infantry mixed in with them to surround the enemy's left wing, which stands opposite himself and press it constantly from the rear.'[12] It is patently obvious that if Valens were in this position then he would have been very exposed to attack once the Gothic cavalry swept away his right wing cavalry. This explained why Ammianus stated that:

While all scattered in flight over unknown paths, the emperor, hedged about by dire terrors, and slowly treading over heaps of corpses, took refuge with the Lancers ('*lancearios*', the '*Lanciarii*') and the Mattiarii, who, so long as the vast numbers of the enemy could be sustained, had stood unshaken with bodies firmly planted. On seeing him Trajanus cried that all hope was gone, unless the emperor, abandoned by his body-guard, should at least be protected by his foreign auxiliaries. On hearing this the general called Victor hastened to bring quickly to the emperor's aid the Batavi, who had been posted not far off as a reserve force; but when he could find none of them, he retired and went away. And in the same way Richomeres and Saturninus made their escape from danger.

The two units Valens sought refuge with are likely to have been the *Lanciarii Seniores* and the *Mattiarii Iuniores*; two crack Palatine Legions who had served with distinction during Julian's Sassanid campaign. The Notitia notes that they were part of the eastern army which Valens would have commanded. Valens, who may or may not have remained on his horse at this point, made his way towards his left where the two crack legions were still maintaining the line. They were not held in reserve, as the *Primani* Legion had been at Argentoratum as evidenced by the fact that Trajanus, observing that Valens had fled to the safety of those two legions without the protection of his bodyguard, who appeared to have deserted him, called out for assistance from the auxiliaries posted as a reserve. Victor heard Trajanus' plea and 'hastened to bring quickly to the emperor's aid the Batavi'. The Batavi are mentioned a number of times within Ammianus' history and appear to have served with distinction at a number of battles although they are recorded as performing so badly at one battle that they had to plead not to be disbanded.[13] They may well be the *Auxilia Palatina* unit mentioned in the Notitia and who were normally brigaded with either the Heruli or *Regii Auxilia Palatina* units (see Chapter Fifteen). However, the Batavi could not be found, they had fled the battlefield apparently along with the fleeing cavalry and the rest of the infantry reserves. Victor, taking stock of the perilous situation of the army, and there being no longer reserves to assist Valens or the rest of the infantry for that matter, also left the battlefield. At some point in the battle both Richomeres and another senior officer, Saturninus, also 'made their escape from danger' and left Valens to his fate. Richomeres probably got swept along by the flight of the right wing cavalry and elected to make his escape to safety rather than return to the battlefield.

Ammianus gives a chilling, graphic account of what happened next.

> And so the barbarians, their eyes blazing with frenzy, were pursuing our men, in whose veins the blood was chilled with numb horror; some fell without knowing who struck them down, others were buried beneath the mere weight of their assailants: some were slain by the sword of a comrade; for though they often rallied, there was no ground given, nor did anyone spare those who retreated. Besides all this, the roads were blocked by many who lay mortally wounded, lamenting the torment of their wounds; and with them also mounds of fallen horses filled the plains with corpses. To these ever irreparable losses, so costly to the Roman state, a night without the bright light of the moon put an end.

So, the Roman army finally broke and attempted to make their way to safety. It appears that some made an orderly retreat, standing their ground when hard pressed, but they just could not stem the tide of Gothic warriors. And here in the text there is yet another mention of the roads near to the battlefield, although they were hardly of any use containing as they did a tangled mass of the dead or dying. The cause of the Romans finally giving up and fleeing was the onset of the night as the darkness would have presented the only means of escape, and one cannot blame or fault the overwhelmed Roman troops for attempting to escape when the opportunity presented itself.

What happened to Valens when his was army routed? This perhaps will never be known for no one appears to have seen what happened to him. Ammianus tells it thus:

> At the first coming of darkness the emperor, amid the common soldiers as was supposed (for no one asserted that he had seen him or been with him), fell mortally wounded by an arrow, and presently breathed his last breath; and he was never afterwards found anywhere. For since a few of the foe were active for long in the neighbourhood for the

purpose of robbing the dead, no one of the fugitives or of the natives ventured to approach the spot. The Caesar Decius, we are told, met a similar fate; for when he was fiercely fighting with the barbarians and his horse, whose excitement he could not restrain, stumbled and threw him, he fell into a marsh, from which he could not get out, nor could his body be found. Others say that Valens did not give up the ghost at once, but with his bodyguard (*candidatis*) and a few eunuchs was taken to a peasant's cottage near by, well fortified in its second storey; and while he was being treated by unskilful hands, he was surrounded by the enemy, who did not know who he was, but was saved from the shame of captivity. For while the pursuers were trying to break open the bolted doors, they were assailed with arrows from a balcony of the house; and fearing through the inevitable delay to lose the opportunity for pillage, they piled bundles of straw and firewood about the house, set fire to them, and burned it men and all. From it one of the bodyguards leaped through a window, but was taken by the enemy; when he told them what had happened, he filled them with sorrow at being cheated of great glory, in not having taken the ruler of the Roman Empire alive. This same young man, having later escaped and returned secretly to our army, gave this account of what had occurred. When Spain had been recovered, with a similar disaster the second of the Scipios, we are told, was burned with a tower in which he had taken refuge and which the enemy had set on fire. This much, at any rate, is certain, that neither Scipio nor Valens had the fortune of burial which is death's final honour.

It is interesting that this implies that Valens' clothing and armour did not single him out as being the Emperor, and that his appearance was the same as the rest of his troops. It was widely rumoured that he had not perished on the battlefield but had been escorted by his bodyguard, and some eunuchs, to a fortified farm building where they attempted to treat his wound. Not only Ammianus, but Jordanes, Socrates, Sozomen and Zosimus all tell versions of this tale.[14] The Goths discovered that there were Roman troops in the building but were unaware of the presence of Valens; when they could not persuade the Romans to leave, instead being greeted by a hail of arrows by the defenders, the Goths set light to the building, killing Valens in the process. Whilst Ammianus lamented the fact that Valens had perished in the flames and had not had the 'fortune of burial', most of the other accounts felt that it was a case of 'divine wrath' that he perished by fire!

And so perished Valens, along with Trajanus and Sebastianus, Aequitius and Valerianus; thirty-five Tribunes also fell including Potentius the son of Ursicinus, one of Constantius II's most illustrious commander-in-chiefs. What was worse was that 'barely a third part' of the Roman army managed to escape and this would have a profound impact in the decades to come. As Ammianus so tragically put it, 'The annals record no such massacre of a battle except the one at Cannae.'

The infantry who broke scattered 'some to the right, others to the left, or wherever their fear took them'. A large proportion headed back to Adrianople where the Roman camp and the city walls would offer them protection.

In concluding this chapter I believe I can now draw up a timetable of events of the Battle of Adrianople as shown below:

1. The Roman army left Adrianople at approximately 6.00 am. The baggage train was left behind in the camp, indicating that Valens did not expect to fight a battle that day.
2. The army marched initially over rough terrain or by winding paths but at some stage they approached the Gothic wagon laager by a road or roads. It was travelling in a column at least eight miles long.
3. The Roman army was marching with part of the cavalry on its right flank whilst the rest of the cavalry were marching with the infantry, indicating that something to their left was protecting that flank, probably the Tonzos River.
4. The Roman scouts sighted the Gothic encampment at a distance of eight miles into the march. The column was travelling at a speed of 3 miles an hour and arrived at approximately 10.00 am and was fully deployed around the Gothic camp by approximately 1.00 pm. Alternatively, the column was taking a longer route or travelling at a rate of only 1.5/2 miles an hour on average, instead of the more usual 4 miles an hour. If this was the case then this indicated that the route the army took was either very rough, delaying their rate of travel, or they took a route that was much longer than the quickest route to the Gothic encampment.

5. The Goths had formed up their wagons in a circle, not as a series of barricades or a semi-circle, such as others have claimed.

6. The Roman army deployed with the sun behind them, indicating they were facing north/north-east.

7. The Roman army was fully deployed and ready for battle by the time Valens and Fritigern entered into negotiations.

8. Richomeres set off behind the Roman right flank with the *Scutarii* and *Sagittarii* cavalry guard units as an escort. It was these units that initially engaged the Goths before then fleeing the battlefield, taking the rest of the Roman right wing cavalry with them.

9. The main Gothic attack, initiated by the flight of the two guard cavalry units, began on the Roman right wing, probably around 4.00 pm.

10. The Roman left wing infantry managed to reach the wagons and were engaging the Goths. The infantry were forced to retreat and move to their right when the Roman cavalry to their left fled the battlefield. This indicates that part of the Gothic cavalry force had made its way around the back of the wagons to attack the Roman left wing, or another group of Gothic cavalry coming from the north-west attacked that wing by surprise.

11. Valens was stationed on the Roman right wing, or between the infantry and the cavalry to their right. Valens then headed towards his left for the perceived safety of the legions that were stationed in the centre of the Roman army when the Gothic cavalry routed the Roman cavalry on the right wing.

12. The Roman infantry on the left were forced right towards the Roman centre by the combined Gothic cavalry and infantry assault.

13. The Roman infantry held in reserve fled the battlefield, probably as a result of seeing the Roman cavalry on both wings leaving the battlefield.

14. The Roman army continued fighting until nightfall, approximately 8.00 pm, when the remaining Roman infantry finally routed and fled for safety under the cover of darkness. Some of them reached Adrianople where the residents initially refused them entry.

15. Valens was caught up in the rout and either perished with those who were cut down by the pursuing Goths, or was wounded and taken to a fortified farmhouse where he was burnt to death.

16. Whilst some notable officers were able to make their escape, including Victor and Richomeres, the loss of experienced generals such as Sebastianus and Trajanus, along with a large number of Tribunes and other officers, plus the loss of two thirds of the army was to have a major impact on future campaigns.

Chapter Twelve

Aftermath

Night brought an end to the slaughter of the Roman army. Valens either lay dead on the battlefield or was being besieged in a local farmhouse before meeting a grisly end. The remnants of his army were scattered, some hid in the hills and woods nearby, and most were fleeing down the roads and byways towards Adrianople. It's not hard to imagine how the victorious Goths spent the night. They would have plundered the fallen Romans of their weapons and armour, and then celebrated in their tribe's fashion, praising the martial prowess of Fritigern and offering thanks to their ancestors and to God. However, by daybreak they were on the move, determined to reach Adrianople and take it by storm. Deserters and captured prisoners had informed the Goths that the Court officials, Valens' imperial insignia, and the imperial treasury were all located at Adrianople. According to Ammianus the Goths had encircled Adrianople 'at the fourth hour of the day'.[1] This would have been approximately 9.00 am. This would have meant that if the Goths had indeed left at daybreak, approximately 6.00 am, they would have covered the distance from their encampment in just three hours, whereas the previous day the Romans may have taken at least seven hours to reach the Gothic encampment, a fact that has not been commented on before and raises many questions, not least why didn't the Romans the previous day take the same route to the Gothic encampment which would have taken probably only half the time to get there? As I discussed in the previous chapter, the Romans took the shortest route to the Gothic encampment and were fully deployed by 1.00 pm. Or they took a route where they hoped to approach from a direction the Goths were not expecting them to approach from, but was a much longer one. Or the Roman army took a route which afforded the army some protection, i.e. by initially following the Tonzos River north before the army turned north-east towards the Goth encampment, which also was a longer route than they could have taken.

If the Goths had thought that the defeat of the Romans the previous day would lead to a similar victory at the city itself they were in for a very rude awakening. Many of the survivors from the battle had not been allowed entry inside the city and were taking shelter in buildings close by to the walls. The citizens of Adrianople were no doubt suspicious of those outside the walls, and of course they were deserters from the battle and did not deserve the protection of the city walls. These survivors, aided by missile fire from the walls, put up a stout resistance which lasted 'until the ninth hour of the day' (approximately 2.00 pm). Without warning 300 of the Roman defenders down by the walls broke ranks and went over to the Goths. They no doubt believed the Goths were going to welcome them with open arms but to their surprise the deserters were instead seized by the Goths and butchered to a man. The Romans watching from above and below the walls took note and there were no further desertions! A sudden thunderstorm then sprang up and put paid to the conflict, the Goths streamed back to their encampment in the pouring rain without having achieved their aim.[2]

An envoy was sent by Fritigern the next day to the city, probably including the same Christian who had carried the letters from Fritigern to Valens. He was not allowed entry into city and he was forced to read the contents of Fritigern's letter from outside the walls. The letter ordered the defenders to hand over the city and upon doing so their lives would be spared. The defenders refused Fritigern's demands and made preparations to defend the city from further attacks.[3] Fritigern then turned to subterfuge to gain access to the city. He ordered some Romans, who had deserted to the side of the Goths after the battle of Adrianople, to make their way to the city as if they had escaped and were fleeing from the Goths. Once inside the city they were to set light to part of it and whilst the defenders were engaged in putting out the fire the Goths, on seeing the smoke and flames, would then be alerted that this ruse had worked and they would then be able to storm the undefended section of the walls and thus take the city. The plan was foiled because although the deserters were admitted back into the city, the defenders became suspicious of the conflicting tales they gave and under torture the deserters confessed as to their true purpose and were executed (Amm, 15, 7–9). The Goths, unaware of this, carried out their preparations for attacking the city and 'before the beginning of the third watch' (approximately 2.00 am) they attempted to storm the city's gates. They were met not with an undefended city but by a storm of missile fire by the alert and waiting defenders. The Goths were further taken aback during the battle when the Romans began to rain down stones from the artillery pieces on the walls and they had to be rallied by their chieftains who attempted to inspire their fellow tribesmen by fighting in the front ranks.[4] The Goths made a concerted effort to scale the walls with specially prepared ladders but these attempts were thwarted when the inhabitants of the city began breaking up columns in the city and throwing down the drums they were made up from on to the Goths below the walls. The battle went on throughout the entire day and when night fell the Goths retired to their temporary camp not far away, having again not achieved their aim of taking the city.[5] The Goths spent the night taking stock of the situation and realizing that they were not going to be able to take Adrianople as they had planned, they decided instead to move to other less well defended cities such as Perinthus, as Roman deserters from the battle several days beforehand had told them the location of that city and others who were not so well defended and also the location of the valuables in those other cities.[6]

Whilst the Goths were attempting to storm Adrianople, Victor, having successfully escaped from the main battlefield, made his way via a long, circuitous route to avoid the Gothic bands now roaming freely through Thrace and in the surrounding provinces. He travelled through Thessaly, Moesia and then to where Gratian was in Pannonia, to bring news of the death and defeat of Valens. Gratian weighed up his options. He could continue east and attack the Goths, who had been badly mauled at the siege of Adrianople, but in doing so he risked a similar fate to Valens, or he could turn around and head back west. It was the latter option he chose and he marched back towards Gaul.[7]

Once the besieging Goths had departed from Adrianople, and scouts that were sent out reported the Goths were no longer in the vicinity, the defenders waited until midnight and then themselves departed. Some went to Macedonia, some to Philippopolis, whilst others must have surely headed to Constantinople. As they still had not heard of the fate of Valens they were no doubt heading to these cities in the desperate attempt to rejoin what possibly remained of the army that had been under Valens' command. They were to find no such army or the presence of the emperor, both were gone.[8]

Fritigern reached Perinthus, but fearing a similar debacle to his previous attempts at storming a city he instead pitched camp nearby and devastated the area around, capturing or slaying anyone who had the misfortune to be found as evidenced in Libanius.[9] He enticed the Alans and Huns in that region to throw in their lot with him with promises of 'wonderful prizes' and he set forth with this combined band on his most audacious venture yet, an attempt on Constantinople itself![10]

Fritigern and his horde rushed towards Constantinople as quickly as they could, expecting no doubt to find little resistance against this unexpected attack. However, Fritigern found that the eastern Romans had acquired a new ally, one whom Fritigern's troops were totally unprepared for. Recently arrived in Constantinople were Saracen cavalry sent by their Queen Mavia. She had recently converted to Christianity and had sent troops to aid Valens with his proposed invasion of the Sassanids. These troops, aided by citizens armed by funds provided by Dominica, wife of Valens, put up a stout defence. The Saracen cavalry were much lighter than their Gothic counterparts and they took advantage of this, darting around the heavier Gothic cavalry and picking them off when they could and then retreating too swiftly for the Goths to catch them before returning and repeating these assaults.[11] The Goths, and indeed the Roman defenders of Constantinople, were at one point astonished by something they witnessed that they had never seen before. As Ammianus relates:

But the oriental troop (*turma*) had the advantage from a strange event, never witnessed before. For one of their number, a man with long hair and naked except for a loin-cloth, uttering hoarse and dismal cries, with drawn dagger rushed into the thick of the Gothic army, and after killing a man applied his lips to his throat and sucked the blood that poured out. The barbarians, terrified by this strange and monstrous sight, after that did not show their usual self-confidence when they attempted any action, but advanced with hesitating steps.[12]

This horrifying event, added to the fact that Fritigern's men had absolutely no chance of storming a city the size of Constantinople, especially when they were unable to storm one the size of Adrianople, led to Fritigern ordering the siege equipment he had brought along destroyed and then they departed to spread death and destruction all across the northern provinces as far as the Julian Alps.[13]

The next act, whilst seen through our eyes must appear extremely callous and barbaric, must be tempered with the fact that those were desperate times, requiring equally desperate measures. With no emperor on the eastern throne, for Theodosius had not yet been elevated to that position by Gratian, somebody had to deal with a potential disaster falling upon the eastern cities. When the Goths first approached Valens two years before, hostages had been taken comprised of children of the various Gothic chieftains and nobles. These had been scattered around the eastern cities so that they could be easily confined. And Valens had been recruiting from them for his upcoming planned invasion of Sassanid Persia, even when the Goths had been rebelling. There were hundreds, if not thousands, of Goths stationed all over the east, and all potentially could join in with their rebellious kinsmen once they learnt of Valens' death and defeat. It fell to Julius, *Magister Militum trans Taurus* (Commander-in-Chief of the troops beyond the Taurus), to take temporary charge and deal with the issue. He petitioned the Senate at Constantinople to authorize him to carry out action that would prevent the eastern cities falling into the hands of the Goths. The action he proposed was this – he would write letters to the leaders of the cities ordering them that at a certain day and time they were to gather the Goths together in a public place, using the bait of overdue pay as a way of enticing them to comply with this instruction. Troops were to be positioned on the roofs of the buildings overlooking the places the Goths were gathered and at a prearranged signal, the raising of a banner, the troops were to shoot arrows and slingshot at the Goths below them. The plan worked exactly as Julius had ordered, the Goths in all the cities of the east were slaughtered to a man. The threat to the east had now been removed.[14]

The year AD 378 drew to a close with the Goths, Huns and Alans undefeated, no emperor on the eastern throne and the western one settled in Gaul pondering what to do next. A deep pause was settling over the two halves of the Roman Empire, and no one knew what the future held.

It is not my intention to discuss in any depth the events from the accession to the eastern throne on 19 January AD 379 of Theodosius, one time military commander who had been retired during the reign of Valentinian to an estate in Spain, that is the task of another author. Instead I will end my work as Ammianus did, before the accession of Theodosius to the throne of the east.

I will mention that the Goths forced changes upon the Roman Empire that were to have long-lasting effects. Roman law had to be in some cases rewritten or changed, and new laws had to be introduced.[15] Sections of the Empire were only nominally under the control of the emperors, and the Huns were beginning to make their presence felt south of the Danube.

Before leaving this chapter it is worth noting that whilst the defeat at Adrianople was indeed a mighty blow to the Romans, at the time contemporary writers did not really consider it was a fatal one. Themistius, Libanius, Gregory of Nyssa, Ambrose of Milan etc., all writing shortly after the battle took place initially appeared to be positive, believing that the Romans would prevail over the barbarians like they had done in the past; it was just a matter of rebuilding the army.[16] However, there appeared to be a sense that perhaps this may not be the case by the time Ammianus wrote his history, around AD 395, because he stated that the Battle of Adrianople was on a scale equal to that of Cannae. Ammianus would have been acutely aware that by the time he was completing the final book of his history that the Goths had been on Roman soil for nearly twenty years and there was scant evidence of them being ejected. It was obvious by the time that Vegetius was writing that the Goths were staying put within the Western Empire, and the Empire was tottering; by the time Zosimus wrote his history the Western Empire had collapsed under pressure from barbarian tribes who lived north of the Rhine and Danube. And once it became apparent that the Goths were not going to be ejected from the Empire the blame game started. The blame for the defeat at Adrianople was levelled firmly at the feet of Valens, also to blame were some of his officers, the bad advice he was given, the ineptitude of the soldiers and Valens' worship of Arian Christianity. No one pointed the finger at perhaps the real culprit of the defeat at Adrianople, and that was of course Fritigern. It's a mystery why even modern authors have missed the fact that if Fritigern had indeed intended to enter into a treaty with Valens on the day of the battle then the battle that broke out was due to his losing control of his cavalry. Yes, the *Scutarii* and *Sagittarii* attacked the Goths, but they may have genuinely thought that the Goths that they encountered when escorting Richomeres to the camp were about to attack them. It's as if the gods conspired to ensure that no matter what happened that day a battle would break out.

A final note – just thirty-two years after Adrianople, Rome, the Eternal City, was sacked by Goths led by Alaric, a Goth who had risen to the rank of *Magister* in the western army. Ninety-eight years after the battle another Goth, Odovacar, deposed the last Roman Emperor of the west, Romulus Augustulus, leaving only the eastern emperor to rule over what remained of the rest of the Roman Empire.

That is perhaps the lasting legacy of the Goths.

Chapter Thirteen

'What If ...'

The Battle of Adrianople and the events leading up to it lend themselves to a number of intriguing 'what if' questions. Any of the below 'what if's' could potentially have happened and I will discuss those which in my opinion could have happened had the circumstances been right.

What If – Valentinian had still been alive?

For me this is the most intriguing question of all of the 'what if's'. Valentinian died just a year before the Goths appeared on the banks of the Danube and before they were admitted into the Empire. What would have been the position had Valentinian still been alive? From what we know of Valentinian and his personality, I think it can be safely said he would have vehemently opposed the Goths being permitted to cross the Danube. He would have strongly advised Valens to deny the Goths entry and under no circumstances should they be permitted south of the Danube. Had the Goths forced their way over then the likelihood would have been Valentinian would have ordered Valens to gather his forces and march against them whilst at the same time Valentinian would have marched with the western army to join his brother. Had Valens ignored Valentinian then I suspect Valentinian would have marched against Valens and attempted to permanently remove him as emperor, leaving Valentinian as emperor of the west and he would have installed Gratian as co-emperor of the east. Had the Goths not been permitted to cross the Danube they would either have had to submit to the Huns or risk crossing the Danube against a hostile Roman reception. Either way neither of these options would have looked good for the Goths and it's likely that their impact on Roman history would have been far less as a result. Had Valens let the Goths cross in defiance of Valentinian's instructions then either Valentinian would have sought Valens' removal by peaceful means, assassination or by force of arms on the battlefield. Had Valens gone quietly then Valentinian would have become sole emperor and may have remained so, he after all only became co-emperor at the insistence of the army and did not initially appear too keen to share the Empire with Valens, or anyone else, come to that. If Valens refused to leave then Valentinian may have tried his method of inviting Valens to a banquet under the pretext of wishing to discuss the issue, then having Valens killed. If Valens did not fall for this ploy, which he may well not have done knowing as he did that being invited to a banquet was likely to be injurious to the health, then Valentinian may have sent an assassin to deal with Valens; again, in this scenario Valentinian would have become sole emperor as if Valens had gone peacefully. If he did not or if Valens survived the assassination attempt then the only choice left would have been a civil war between the two brothers. In that scenario there were three possible outcomes: Valens was defeated and killed either in battle or at some stage afterwards, Valentinian was defeated and killed either in battle or at some stage afterwards or both brothers were killed, leaving the Empire in complete turmoil. Any battle between the two would have been interesting because Valens would have naturally called upon the Goths to support him, it was after all in their best interest to do so, and Valentinian could have called upon the Alamanni King Macrianus to supply him with troops from the Alamanni tribes that were allied to Valentinian.

If Valentinian had been the victor then the outcome for the Goths would have been dire. I could see Valentinian forcibly making them return north of the Danube or enslaving them; his history against other barbarian tribes was the surest indicator of the action he would have taken. Had that happened then Roman history as we know it would have taken a far different course. If the unthinkable had happened and Valens had defeated Valentinian then again Roman history may well have taken a much different course, the Goths would have been peacefully settled in Thrace as a reward for their support and Valens would have been free to put his plans for invading Sassanid Persia in to full motion, with thousands of Gothic recruits to swell his armies' ranks. What he would have done with Gratian is moot, he may have elevated him to be co-emperor but with aides who would have ensured he was kept in line. If the worst case scenario of both Valentinian and Valens dying on the battlefield had happened then one probable outcome would have been Gratian would have been proclaimed as emperor of the West but there would have been any number of usurpers coming out of the woodwork, not only trying for the Eastern throne but also for the Western one. It would be like the Crisis of the Third Century all over again but this time with barbarians on Roman soil and others such as the Huns, Alans, Franks, Alamanni and even the Sassanids taking advantage of the chaos. How the Empire would have fared under these circumstances is anybody's guess.

What If – The Goths had not rebelled?

Again a rather intriguing question. If the Goths had not been so ill-treated by Lupicinus and Maximus during their crossing over the Danube then they would have moved to their new homeland in Thrace where they would have remained peacefully farming the land and providing willing recruits for the Roman army. Valens would have used the Goths to swell the ranks of the three armies he was raising to invade Sassanid Persia and by AD 378 he would have been ready to launch that invasion. How large his invasion force would have been is of course open to question, but with three whole armies at his disposal I would suggest a figure from 60,000 to 90,000 strong would not be too far from the mark. And what's more important, Valens would have many more cavalry at his disposal than any other Roman army had ever had, courtesy of the Greuthungi Goths. The outcome of his invasion is of course purely conjecture here but I would like to think it would have been far more successful than Julian's attempt over thirty years beforehand. The Romans would also have been able to put up a greater resistance to the Huns and Alans when they swept south-eastwards towards the Danube frontier, not having to expend troops fighting the Goths. Who knows, but what would history now be like if Valens had not had to fight the Goths, successfully invaded Sassanid Persia, defeated Sharpur and prevented the Huns and the other tribes from crossing the Danube?

What If – The Goths had negotiated a treaty at the city of Adrianople and the battle never took place?

This outcome could well have happened had Valens agreed to the terms laid out in the letter sent the night before the Battle. He could have asked for, and been given, a truce by Fritigern and a new treaty negotiated. The Goths would have been settled in Thrace as they requested and Valens would have got his recruits for his army. The outcome would then have in all probability been the same had the Goths not rebelled as discussed above.

What If – A treaty had been negotiated at the battlefield and the Romans had not attacked the Goths?

Again, had not the returning Gothic cavalry been attacked by the Romans, the treaty negotiations between the two sides would have continued. Valens and Fritigern were at the point of exchanging hostages when the attack took place, Richomeres was actually riding towards the Gothic wagons when the cavalry escorting him clashed with the Gothic cavalry. Had both sides not fought then it would have been the same outcome as discussed, the Goths settled in Thrace and Valens invading Sassanid Persia.

What If – Valens had defeated the Goths at Adrianople?

In a way this is both the easiest, yet most difficult 'what if' question. The easiest answer of course is that had Valens defeated the Goths at Adrianople then their impact on Roman history would have probably come to an end. He would have forced the survivors to settle anywhere he chose to do so, and he would have enslaved and forcibly enrolled many into service and the army. If Fritigern had survived the battle and been captured he would have been forced to convince the rest of the Goths south of the Danube to bend to the Roman will and accede to Valens' demands. He may well have been allowed to live as there does seem to be a sort of bond between himself and Valens, he did after all convert to Christianity as thanks for Valens' support against Athanaricus and he did not leave Thrace during the time the Goths first crossed the Danube in AD 376. Had Fritigern been killed then no doubt Valens would have installed a pliable Gothic chieftain over the Goths to ensure they toed the line. Had Fritigern survived and escaped the battlefield then he may have been able to rally the rest of the Goths still within Roman territory, and could potentially have continued the war against Valens with support from the Huns and Alans. Valens' position would have been much stronger though, and with support from Gratian he may have finally defeated Fritigern in a future battle and put paid to the Goths, who would have ended up just being a footnote in any future history.

What If – Valens had waited for Gratian and his army to arrive?

Another interesting one, because had Valens waited for Gratian to arrive, and my calculation of how far way he was puts him at between four and seven days' march away, then his combined force would certainly have outnumbered that of Fritigern. If he had waited then Valens could have continued the negotiations with Fritigern, and also been able to keep that chieftain and his fellow tribesmen under constant surveillance. Fritigern would have had to make some stark choices, agree to whatever terms Valens wished to impose upon him or risk a battle, which in all probability the Goths would have lost. Hindsight of course is a wonderful thing, and had Valens only waited a few more days then the whole course of Roman, and probably western European history would have changed and nothing we know now would be the same.

Chapter Fourteen

The Location of the Battle of Adrianople

The location of the Battle of Adrianople has, up to the date of the publication of this book, not been discovered. McDowell believes the Gothic camp was near to the modern village of Muratcali, Turkey, approximately ten miles north-east from Edirne (Adrianople). Runkel locates it near to modern Demirhanli, whilst I have provided a quote earlier stating that the Gothic camp was at the twelfth milestone, approximately eleven miles away from Adrianople, but the direction unknown.

Wherever the Gothic camp was, it must have been close to a source of clean drinking water, such as a stream or river. This would give credence to McDowell's placing the camp near Muratcali as there is a stream that runs from north to south on its west side and it's only a short distance east from the Tonzos River. If Valens wanted to take a route that would have involved approaching the Goths from a direction they were not expecting then following the course of the Tonzos River would be an ideal way of doing this. Marching north-west and then following the riverbank north would have allowed the troops to take water directly from the river, and would have negated the need to take the baggage train along. However, using Google Earth, one can see that if an army were to follow the river it is fairly flat on the banks as far as the village of Degimenyeni, and probably would not hinder the army much. The army could then turn north-east and head through what appears to be a plain towards Muratcali, again not hindering the army too much one would have thought. The area around Degimenyeni and Muratcali is heavy with cultivated fields and probably was during the Late Roman period, again likely to make it easier to march rather than more difficult. However, as Donnelly stated, Ammianus' text could be read as the army was travelling along winding paths, which following a meandering river would have been the case. And following the river would have almost doubled the length of the journey the army would have had to travel to reach the Gothic camp. The army did travel by road for at least the last part of their march towards the Gothic encampment. This section of the march may have been of several hours' duration during which the army may have had no access to water, and what water the troops had managed to fill up in their personal water containers was probably used up by the time they reached the wagons, and that's the reason Ammianus stated the army was suffering from thirst. Just to the south of Muratcali, and also to the south of the village of Buyukdolluk, Google Earth shows there are some very interesting circular shapes in the ploughed fields that could, just could, be indicative of where a circular camp or camps have been made in the past. They are situated just off the road leading south from Muratcali and the road south-west from Buyukdolluk. We know from Claudian that the Goths after Adrianople did construct camps with a ditch and palisade, and whilst Donnelly argues that this would be for more permanent encampments, Fritigern had been exposed to Roman methods of laying out camps when Valens sent the army of Thrace to support Fritigern's civil war against Athanaricus. This may well have led to Fritigern incorporating some Roman camp elements within their normal wagon encampments. The only drawback to this suggestion that the rings show the possible site of the Gothic camp is that Buyukdolluck is less than eight miles' distance from Edirne, far too close for the army to have taken over six hours to travel there. Unless of course the army followed the river before taking the road north-east. Perhaps the markings in those fields are from Gothic camps set up when Fritigern turned from heading towards Nike and moving south-west towards Adrianople?

If Valens had marched due north from the east side of Adrianople, where it's entirely likely his camp was pitched, then his army would have passed through a lot of rough ground with little evidence of a usable road until you reach the village of Buyukdolluk and then turn north-east along the road to Muratcali. If the army travelled almost due east there is a main highway passing near to Demirhanli, this appears to run fairly straight towards Istanbul (Constantinople) and is probably built over the old Constantinople to Adrianople Roman highway. This may have meant a march overland to that area, and part of it does indeed appear to be rough going with a number of streams blocking the way. However, again, this would have meant that the troops would have had a number of opportunities to fill up on water, providing of course that the streams existed in AD 378, and that they do not dry up in the summer months. The issues with setting the battle near Demirhanli are that it would have made more tactical sense for Valens to have camped near to Demirhanli, which appears to have been near to the old Roman road, and also may have been very close to Nike, if not Nike itself. Once he marched from Melanthias, rather than travel onwards to Adrianople it would have made more sense for the army to camp at Nike. This would then have afforded a shorter distance to travel north with the army to reach the Goths, rather than march to Adrianople and then back eastwards again. Had Valens camped at Nike it would have prevented the Goths moving closer to Nike or even towards Constantinople. Other candidates for the location of the battlefield could be the area lying between Korucu to the north and Ortakci to the north-east. This area has a lot of rough terrain along with sources of water near the towns and also a few areas of cultivation and places where armies could set up camps or deploy. Two prime candidates for the battle location in this area are the villages of Sinankoy and Ortakci as movement through these two areas would have taken the Goths away from most inhabited areas on their move down from Kabyle. There are some streams nearby, and there are roads that led up to both villages. The evidence is then that the most likely candidates for the location of the battlefield are the villages of Muratcali, Sinakoy or Ortakci. All three require travelling over rough terrain or winding paths to reach them at least partway along the route, all lack access to water along the route for at least the last few miles, and all have roads that lead to them on the last part of the journey. Wherever the battle took place it was reachable within less than half a day's march had the army taken the most direct route (see diagram 1 for the locations discussed above and distances noted from modern Edirne, site of ancient Adrianople).

One important caveat about attempting to locate the site of the battlefield is that a series of very powerful earthquakes have occurred in this region over the centuries and this may well have caused the topography to have changed beyond recognition from that in AD 378. The land mass may have risen and fallen in places, streams and rivers changed course or dried up altogether etc. It will probably be the case that a very lucky archaeological find may be the only way of finding the location of the battle now.

Chapter Fifteen

The Roman Empire and its Army During the Reign of Valens

The Roman Empire when Valens became Emperor was in many ways both the same, yet very different, to the Empire several centuries before. A person from the second century who had somehow managed to travel to the future would have recognized much of the artistic works and building styles, yet the people surrounding him would have been the most noticeable difference. By the middle of the fourth century the Empire was home to a diverse and multicultural group of peoples. As the Empire stretched from Hadrian's Wall in Britain to the Euphrates River far to the east so did the peoples within the borders reflect this expanse. Walking down the streets of any city within the Empire one might encounter Sarmatians, Sassanid Persians, Britons, Alamanni, Franks, Saxons, Vandals, and Goths etc. amongst the common Roman citizenry. This population make up was reflected within the ranks of the army as well.

Diocletian began the reformation of the Roman Empire, introducing a western and eastern emperor, known as Augustus, with a junior emperor, Caesar, whose role would be to replace the Augustus when he stepped down at the proper time. This was known as the Tetrarchy and it lasted between AD 284–AD 305. Diocletian also divided the Empire into almost a hundred provinces. These provinces were governed by Proconsuls; under these were the *Consulares*, then the *Correctores* and finally the *Praesides*. The provinces themselves were grouped into *Dioceses*, overseen by a *Vicarius*, who oversaw their affairs. The exceptions to this were the proconsuls and the urban prefect of Rome, and later on in Constantinople, who were directly subordinate to the two Augustus' and the two Caesars.

Information on the *Dioceses* and Provinces, those who governed them and the military units stationed there are contained within the rather enigmatic document known as the *Notitia Dignitatum* (Record of Offices). This document is dated to around AD 420 for the western section and AD 390 for the eastern section. The *Notitia* is a favourite of re-enactors and wargamers because it shows the shield patterns of many of the infantry and cavalry units that served in the Late Roman field armies. Whilst it is very useful for locating where the officials were based, unfortunately many of the units in the document appear in both eastern and western sections, probably as a result of cross postings, so stating exactly where a unit was based can be difficult due to this. The *Notitia* also shows the location of the various high ranking military officers and the armies they commanded.

The Tetrarchy system failed due to the inability of the emperors to agree to hand over power to their Caesars and civil war broke out. From the dust arose Constantine I, who would be known afterwards as 'The Great'. He became sole emperor and instituted other reforms. In AD 318, he brought in an administrative system in the form of Praetorian Prefectures. The holders of these posts were rotated on a frequent basis and they did not have a co-colleague to assist them as was the case in the Tetrarchy they replaced. Constantine built a new city on the former city of Byzantium, this became known as Constantinople. Constantinople was the permanent seat of the government of the eastern half of the Empire. Rome had by this time become just the symbolic head of the Empire and various other cities became the imperial seat of government including Trier and Mediolanum.

The Empire was briefly divided once more between the sons of Constantine but again civil war and strife led to an eventual victor, Constantius II, who became sole emperor by AD 350. Constantius elevated his nephew Gallus to Caesar of the East in AD 351 when it became clear that the Empire could no longer be solely ruled by one person. Gallus so abused his position that Constantius had him executed in AD 354 and in AD 355 he promoted his nephew Julian to Caesar. This relationship broke down and civil war loomed again but before both sides could clash Constantius died on route; he named Julian as his successor on his deathbed. Julian had no intention of sharing the Empire with anyone else and he ruled as sole emperor until his death on the battlefield against the Sassanids in June AD 363. The army promoted Jovian to the throne but his reign was very short-lived and in AD 364 the army promoted Valentinian to the throne.

When Valens was acclaimed as emperor in AD 365 the Empire was at its greatest extent, only the northern section of the former province of Dacia, abandoned long before, and some small territories ceded to the Sassanids in the East were missing, but overall the Empire was larger than it had ever been. As shown in Chapter Three Valentinian divided the Empire between himself and Valens, Valentinian ruling from Trier whilst Valens' seat was Constantinople.

Another major change during this period was in connection with religion within the Empire and the rise of Christianity as the pre-eminent form of worship. Christianity was a minor cult by the time of Diocletian and it may have vanished altogether had it not been for the conversion of Helena, Constantine's mother, to that faith. She was zealous in her devotion to the Christian faith and her influence over her son in religious matters cannot be overestimated. Constantine himself only converted on his deathbed, but his sons, Constantine II, Constans and Constantius, became committed Christians. On becoming sole emperor, Constantius began purges against the other religions within the Empire, ordering temples to be closed, others torn down and the persecution of their worshippers. There was a brief reversal of this policy when Julian ascended to the purple. He may have been studying to become a Christian priest before he became Caesar but his obvious Pagan leaning took over in full force once he ruled the Empire. He attempted to restore the old Pagan beliefs, not entirely successfully as many within the Empire were now dedicated Christians. He carried out limited purges against the Christians and it's probably fortunate for Christianity that he did not rule for long. Valens and his brother Valentinian were committed Christians although they did retain the old Pagan title of *Pontifex Maximus* on their accessions to their respective thrones. Both emperors meddled constantly in religious affairs, much to the obvious disgust of those such as Ammianus and others who commented on this.[1]

Diocletian also separated military from civil command at the lowest, provincial level. The governors of provinces along the frontiers no longer commanded the military forces in their provinces; instead the command of those forces was given to military officers called *Duces Limitis* (Commander of the Border). Although *Duces* normally commanded the forces in a single province, some controlled more than one province. Diocletian's reforms also included the exclusion of the senatorial class from all senior military commands and from all top administrative posts, with the exception of those in Italy itself. Constantine continued the reforms instituted by Diocletian by introducing a new higher officer rank of '*Comes*' (Count). The two highest ranking of the military *Comes* were the *Magister Equitum* (Master of the Horse) and the *Magister Peditum* (Master of the Foot). The lower officer ranks were also reformed. The highest ranking of these was the *Tribunus*, of whom Ammianus was one. These officers commanded both the old and new style units of both the legions and the auxila. The *Praefectus* was an officer who commanded the old style border legions along the frontiers; they could command several units at once if needed. There was another officer rank known as the *Protectores* who were initially created by the Emperor Gallienus as a form of personal bodyguard but who in time became a kind of officer recruiting school from where men such as Ammianus, who were, as a junior officer, once a member of the *Protectores Domestici*, the personal military attendants of the emperor, groomed to become senior officers. Other officer ranks were reformed and included the *Praepostitus* who originally was an officer in temporary command of a unit but by the time Ammianus wrote they either commanded the old style border legions and auxiliary units or it became a title an officer such as a *Tribunus* could be called when commanding a unit. The non-officer ranks were also reformed with the most senior being the *Primicerius* who could take command of his unit if the *Tribunus* was absent, he would then be known as the *Vicarius*. There were other NCOs including the *Ducenarius* who may have commanded 200 men, and the *Centenarius* who Vegetius equated to the old *Centuriones* rank but this is not entirely certain.[2]

It has often been claimed that the Late Roman army relied more and more on 'barbarian' recruits to fill its ranks. In part this was indeed true, a larger army required more men, and those who lived beyond the borders of Rome were more than willing to enrol within the ranks of not only the Auxilia units but also that of the Legions. And the recruits were not just ordinary men, chieftains and kings of various tribes willingly offered their services and many rose to high rank.[3] However, despite the claims of a number of those who have written about both the Late Roman army and the Battle of Adrianople, those who were contemporary with the Battle of Adrianople, such as Ammianus, still considered the army as 'Roman', and manned mostly by 'Romans'.

Along with reforming the officers and NCOs Diocletian began the reformation of the infantry and cavalry units that made up the Roman army. Manpower shortages were solved by the introduction of an annual conscription of Roman citizens for the first time since the days of the Roman Republic. Further, Diocletian may have been responsible for the decree, first recorded in AD 313, which compelled the sons of serving soldiers and veterans to enlist in the army. Diocletian increased the number of the legions, auxilia and other units. To this end he began raising new units and reforming existing ones. He kept some of the old style legions as border defence troops but the other legions and auxilia units were regraded as *Palatine*, *Comitatensis* or *Limitanei*. The *Palatine* units were higher status troops whose role would have originally been troops under the direct command of the emperor. The *Comitatensis* were what would be considered now to be units manned by regular soldiers whilst the *Limitanei* would have been units of a much lower status, generally tasked with providing static defence within a province. In time of need *Limitanei* units could be promoted to field army status where they would then be known as '*Pseudocomitatensis*'. If they remained in the field army long enough the unit could even be promoted to full *Comitatensis* status. The cavalry were similarly made up, with the highest status units being known as the *Scolae*, the rest as *Equites*.

Diocletian further divided both infantry and cavalry units into two halves, which were then known as *Seniores* and *Iuniores*, i.e. the *Lanciarii Seniores* and the *Mattiarii Iuniores* being just two examples. By doing this Diocletian effectively doubled the size of the army although it's not clear if this doubled the number of men in the Late Roman army as the exact number of men in those units is still a matter of debate.[4] Vegetius claimed that the legions up to the reforms of Diocletian were made up of 6,100 infantry and attached to the legion were 726 cavalry. But this must have been the strength on paper, theoretical strength. A number of studies of the Late Roman army have shown that most units were below strength, some seriously so, and it's likely that a legion that was supposed to total 6,100 men probably totalled no more than 5,000–5,500 in reality. Diocletian's reforms may well have included removing the cavalry attached to each legion and forming them into their own, separate units. The same proved true for the artillery that Vegetius stated was attached to each legion, the number of men manning the artillery was eleven per cart-mounted bolt shooting *ballista* (*carroballista*), each legion having fifty-five such pieces, and an unknown number of men manning the larger artillery pieces known as *onagri* ('wild asses'). As it appears the artillery was also removed from the legions and formed into separate units, this would have removed at least another 600–700 men from each legion. This would have further reduced the legion size to down to around the 4,300–4,800 mark. So when Diocletian divided the legions into the *Seniores* and *Iuniores* they may have been between 2,150 and 2,400 men strong. However, this directly conflicts with most modern historians who state that the new style legions that were created were probably no more than 1,200 men strong.[5] My own personal view is that the Late Roman legions were approximately 2,000 strong on average, taking into account the fact that once these newer legions were established they too would have suffered a drop in numbers for the same reasons I have given above. I also base this view on examples in Ammianus where detachments of between 300 and 500 men were taken from each legion for special tasks, such as when Sebastianus was given 300 men from each legion to take with him when he attacked the Goths fleeing from Adrianople in the weeks before the battle of Adrianople itself. If the legions were only 1,200 strong then detaching even 300 men would seriously weaken the legion, as a quarter of it would be away and casualties would further diminish the fighting capabilities of a smaller legion. If the legions were 2,000 men strong then a detachment of 300 or even 500 men would have not had a serious impact on its ability to maintain combat effectiveness. The same debate also applies to the auxilia units. The old style auxilia units still existed but many were stationed on the borders alongside the old style legions that retained their old legionary names and numbering system. First Diocletian and then Constantine raised a new type of auxilia unit, the *Auxilia Palatina*, who had more status than the old style ones. Again, modern historians believe that Auxilia units were approximately 500 men strong, half of the size of the old style Auxilia units. Again, I really cannot believe this and cite the example of Silvanius who in AD 355 travelled through Gaul with 8,000 auxiliaries (Amm XVI, 2, 4). Now, if those Auxilia units were 500 men strong, that would equate to Silvanius travelling with possibly sixteen Auxilia units. The *Notitia Dignitatum* notes that there were only fifteen Auxilia Palatina units in Gaul when it was drawn up, and some of these were raised after Adrianople. Granted some Auxilia units may have been destroyed at Adrianople itself but this still leaves us with the question, did Silvanius really travel through Gaul with all of the *Auxilia Palatina* units stationed there? This is highly unlikely in my opinion. Therefore I would suggest that if the Auxilia were from 800 to 1,000 men strong then that would have meant that Silvanius would have been accompanied by between 8 to 10 Auxilia units, the rest being left to remain in their garrisons. Troops still continued to be stationed along the borders but these older units, often retaining the old style Roman numbering system, had lost much of their status, and many had detachments sent to other provinces and stations. It's likely that these older legions may have retained their original troop strength and may have been around 4,000 men strong if they were at full strength. Other unit types were separate units of *Ballistarii*, which contained artillery pieces of various sizes, units made up of skirmishers and riverine and sea-going troops. The total size of the Roman army during the fourth century is another topic that is hotly debated. John Lydus stated that at the end of the third century AD the army size was 389,704 men. Zosimus gives a figure of 581,000 during the early fourth century whilst Agathias gave a total of 645,000 during the reign of Constantine. The first figure probably relates just to field army strength totals, whilst the last two contain naval, riverine, *limitanae* and other supernumeries. An effective field army strength of 400,000 across the entire Empire does not then seem too large taking these figures into account.

Both legions and Auxilia units were often brigaded together as pairs, for instance the Batavi and the Heruli and the Lanciarii and Mattiarii were noted by Ammianus as doing so.[6] When brigaded together both units would share the same standards. The standards included the usual Vexillum types as well as a new one known as a Draco which was carried by the infantry cohorts.

The organization of the Roman army also underwent a number of changes during the fourth century. These changes, begun during the reign of Diocletian and completed by Constantine, included placing the infantry and cavalry into new style field armies. The reformation of the army during this period led to the creation of three specific army groupings, two of which were technically mobile, the last was a more static defence. These groupings were the *Comitatus Prasentales*, the *Comitatus* and the *Exercitus Limitanei*. The first group were troops that were normally stationed around the imperial capital cities and accompanied the emperor on campaigns. The second group was the more typical regional field army that were stationed within towns, cities and forts within a diocese or province. The last group were generally based in provinces as a static defence.

Originally the *Comitatius Prasentales* field armies would have composed the Palatine units, both Legions and Auxila units. However, over time units of *Comitatensis* made their way into the *Prasentales* field armies, and Palatine troops were posted to the *Comitatus* armies. The size of a typical field army is difficult to gauge but taking some examples into account we can see that they could range from the huge to quite small. During the civil war between Constantius II and Magnentius both emperors raised armies that approached 100,000 men apiece. This would have been at the extreme end of the scale, and in all likelihood these armies were made up of a number of field armies marching together to make a much larger one. Julian's army at Argentoratum was stated as being only between 12,000–15,000 men strong, and Ammianus wrote that it was really not large enough for the task it was allotted. Constantius II campaigned across the Danube against the Sarmatians with an army of 25,000 men; a similar number was assigned to Barbatio, one of his western generals. Julian invaded Sassanid Persia with an army that he divided into two, one part numbering 30,000 men was sent north into Armenia to then move south-east to possibly catch Sharpur in a pincer movement. Taking these numbers into account, a typical field army strength of between 25,000 and 40,000 does not seem too out of place.

The arms and armour of the Late Roman infantry and cavalry were still principally a helmet, body armour, shield, spear and sword, although these now differed from their predecessors. Gone were the elaborate helmets and segmented armour of the previous two centuries. Most troops now wore simple helmets such as the '*intercisa*' type and wore a chain mail hauberk which ended at the elbow and knees. The *pilum* was now almost replaced by a spear called the *spiculum* which was approximately 6½ft long and was able to penetrate armour and also could be thrust to fend off cavalry. A javelin was also carried; it was approximately 3½ft long and called a *verutum*.[7] Other spears that were used were called *hasta* or *lancae*. Shields were either oval or round and were between 2–3ft wide. The infantry carried two swords; the main one was much longer than the *gladius* and was known as the *spatha*. Some troops were also equipped with a new style, hand-hurled weapon called the *mattiobarbuli* or *plumbatae*, more popularly known as darts. They allowed the infantry to inflict casualties at a longer range than the javelin could be thrown. It may be that the Palatine infantry were issued with different body armour and helmets as shown on various monumental works such as the totally destroyed Column of Theodosius and the mostly destroyed Column of Arcadius drawn by a number of artists of varying artistic ability before they were destroyed at some point prior to the seventeenth century. These two columns displayed Theodosius' victory against the Goths in the AD '380s' and Arcadius' victory against the Goths in AD 400. Most of the Roman infantry on those two columns are depicted as wearing muscle cuirasses, with the Goths being shown either unarmoured, as is the case on the Theodosian column, or unarmoured or wearing a mail hauberk on the Arcadian one. The Roman infantry either have a spear which is approximately 6–7ft long or one that appears to be about 3–4ft long. They have shields that were either oval, about 3ft long and 2ft wide, or they are round and about 3ft wide. They have helmets which are mostly of the '*attic*' type with brow guards, although some appear to be wearing types known as '*intercisa*' that were of a much simpler construction. It may be that these works depicted Palatine troops and that these troops were issued muscle cuirasses and Attic helmets as a sign of their status.[8]

The cavalry were made up of four main types, the shield bearing, heavily armoured cavalry called *Equites Catafractarii* armed with a long spear called the *contus* ('barge pole'); the mailed, spear and javelin armed, shield bearing ordinary cavalry called *Equites*; the lighter armoured, javelin armed, shield bearing cavalry known as *Equites Illyricanni* or *Dalmatae*, and the mounted horse archers called *Equites Sagittarii*. Some *Catafractarii* were also known as '*Clibanarii*'. The *Clibanarii* were very heavily armoured, they wore a metal mask that covered the entire face, only the eyes and mouth having holes to see and breathe through. They wore mail armour that covered the rest of the body apart from chest which was covered in a breast plate and the arms and legs that instead had flexible, tubular, metallic armour. Julian and Ammianus stated they did not have shields as their armour made them 'invulnerable' to normal weapons. Their armament was the *contus* and possibly a bow after the manner of the Sassanid *Clibanarii* they were based on. The *Clibanarii* horses were covered in metallic armour, mostly mail and the only vulnerable areas were the bottom of their legs and their underbellies.

Riverine units were used extensively along the Rhine and Danube and they featured during the years AD 376 to AD 378 during Gratian's campaigns and also during the crossing of the Danube by the Goths.

A Roman army of this period would typically form up with the infantry forming the centre and the cavalry equally divided on the flanks of the infantry, the *Catafractii/Clibanarii* being deployed next to the infantry, then the less heavily armoured cavalry with the lighter cavalry and horse archers deployed further out. Whilst the army was deploying for battle the infantry skirmishers, armed with javelins, darts, slings and bows, would screen the deployment and harass the enemy until the signal was given for them to fall behind the main infantry line. There would normally be a reserve line of infantry behind the main line whose task would be to plug any gaps that appeared in the main battle line. Once fully deployed the army would then march forward until they reached the range of their hand-hurled weapons when they would stop. At this point they would trade insults with the enemy and then raise their famous war-cry known as the *barritus*. The infantry would then throw their missile weapons, darts and javelins, whose main effect would probably be to break up the enemy formation and lower the enemy morale. This would then be followed by the signal to engage the enemy in hand to hand combat. At this point the Roman infantry would either lock shields and form a shield wall and brace themselves against the enemy attack, especially if they were facing enemy cavalry, or they would charge forward. The cavalry would attempt to drive any enemy cavalry from the field before then attacking the flanks of the enemy infantry. If all went well and the enemy became broken and routed, the signal would be given to pursue the fleeing enemy troops and it was at this point that most casualties would be caused. If the engagement went against the Romans then the signal for the retreat would be given and they would attempt to make a fighting withdrawal back to their camp if they had one in the vicinity, otherwise they would make for any terrain that provided them with protection or wait for nightfall where the darkness would afford them an opportunity to escape.

A great number of journal and magazine articles, and books, have been written about the Late Roman Empire and its army and I have included in the Bibliography those I consulted whilst researching for this book.

Chapter Sixteen

Biographies

Presented below is a select list of the main characters that had major roles in the events leading up to Adrianople and during the battle itself.

The Romans

Flavius Julius Valens

Born AD 328 at Cibalae in Pannonia. He was the younger brother of Flavius Valentinian, who made Valens his co-emperor, being the second son of Gratianus the Elder. He was one of the '*Protectors Domesticus*' during Julian's campaign and then served Jovian in this role after the death of Julian. How active this early career was is not known, Ammianus and Zosimus hint that his military career at this point was rather nondescript. He was appointed as a '*Tribunus Stabuli*' on 1 March AD 364 and on 28 March 364 was proclaimed 'Augustus' by his brother, now emperor, Valentinian I. He was married to Albia Domnica who bore him three sons. Valens faced a serious problem in AD 365 when Procopius, a relation to Julian, declared himself Augustus in Constantinople. Valens defeated Procopius at the battle of Nacolea in AD 366 after many of Procopius' officers and men changed sides. Procopius fled the battle but was taken to Valens' camp by two of Procopius' officers who despite this were executed along with Procopius. Valens' first Gothic war was instigated by Procopius hiring Goths for his rebel army. During the years AD 371 to AD 372 Valens survived an assassination attempt by Sallustius, one of the Scutarii, and another usurper by the name of Theodorus arose and suffered a similar fate to Procopius. During AD 371 Sharpur II, the King of Kings of Sassanid Persia who had plagued Emperor Constantius II and defeated Julian, began agitating over Armenia. Valens despatched several experienced generals and a large army which defeated the Sassanid army in battle, both sides settling down to an uneasy peace. During AD 373 Valens was involved with the plot to remove the young Armenian King Pap from his throne, an act Ammianus described as 'a terrible crime'. Pap managed to initially escape being captured but was then murdered at a banquet. Relations with the Sassanids broke down again over Armenia and Hiberia and this prompted Valens to attempt to build three armies for his proposed invasion of Sassanid Persia with assistance from the Goths. He also faced revolts in Isauria and by Saracens led by Queen Mavia. The events of AD 376, which saw the arrival of the Goths on the frontier and their subsequent revolt and movement into Roman territory did not appear to have put paid to this dream Valens had of attacking the Sassanids, as Goths were stationed all over the eastern cities in preparation for the proposed invasion as discussed in Chapter Twelve.

Ammianus, who may have met Valens in person, gave a good summing up of Valens' character after his death at Adrianople:

Thus then died Valens, at the age of almost fifty and after a reign of a little less than fourteen years. Of his merits, as known to many, we shall now speak, and of his defects. He was a firm and faithful friend, severe in punishing ambitious designs, strict in maintaining discipline in the army and in civil life, always watchful and anxious lest anyone should elevate himself on the ground of kinship with him; he was excessively slow towards conferring or taking away official positions, very just in his rule of the provinces, each of which he protected from injury as he would his own house, lightening the burden of tributes with a kind of special care, allowing no increase in taxes, not extortionate in estimating the indebtedness from arrears, a harsh and bitter enemy of thievish officials and of those detected in peculation. Under no other emperor does the Orient recall meeting better treatment in matters of this kind. Besides all this, he combined liberality with moderation, and although there are many instances of such conduct, yet it will suffice to set forth one. Since there are always at court some men who are greedy for others' possessions, if anyone, as often happens, claimed a lapsed estate or anything else of the kind, he distinguished clearly between justice and injustice, allowing those who intended to protest a chance to state their case; and if he gave it to the petitioner, he often added as sharers in the gifts gained three or four absentees, to the end that restless people might act with more restraint, when they saw that by this device the gain for which they were so greedy was diminished. As to the public buildings which he restored or built from their very beginning in various cities and towns, in order not to be prolix I say nothing, but leaving this matter to the objects themselves to demonstrate it more obviously than I can. Such conduct is worthy, I think, of emulation by all good men; let me now run through his defects.

He was immoderately desirous of great wealth, and impatient of toil, rather affecting awesome austerity than possessing it, and somewhat inclined to cruelty; he had rather an uncultivated mind, and was trained neither in the art of war nor in liberal studies; he was ready to gain advantage and profit at the expense of others' suffering, and more intolerable when he attributed offences that were committed to contempt of, or injury to, the imperial dignity; then he vented his rage in bloodshed, and on the ruin of the rich. It was unendurable also, that although he wished to appear to refer all controversies and judicial investigations to the laws, and entrusted the examination of such affairs to the regular judges as being specially selected men, nevertheless he suffered nothing to be done contrary to his own caprice. He was in other ways unjust, hot tempered, and ready to listen to informers without distinguishing truth from falsity, a shameful fault, which is very greatly to be dreaded even in these our private affairs of every-day occurrence.

He was a procrastinator and irresolute. His complexion was dark, the pupil of one of his eyes was dimmed, but in such a way as not to be noticed at a distance; his body was well-knit, his height neither above nor below the average; he was knock-kneed, and somewhat pot-bellied.

This will be enough to say about Valens, and it is fully confirmed by the testimony of records contemporary with me. But it is proper not to omit the following story. At the time of the oracle of the tripod, for which, as I have said, Patricius and Hilarius were responsible, he had heard of those three prophetic verses, of which the last is:

When in Mimas' plains the war-god Ares rages.

Being uneducated and rude, he disregarded them at first, but as his very great troubles increased he became abjectly timid, and in recalling that prediction used to shudder at the mention of Asia, where, as he heard from the mouths of learned men, Homer and Cicero have written of a mountain called Mimas, rising above the city of Erythrae. Finally, after his death and the departure of the enemy, it is said that near the place where he was thought to have fallen a monument made of a heap of stones was found, to which was fastened a tablet engraved with Greek characters, showing that a distinguished man of old called Mimas was buried there.

Flavius Richomeres

Place and date of birth unknown. He was a Frank who attained both high military and civil status, serving as *Comes Domesticorum* under Gratian from at least AD 377. Gratian dispatched Richomeres with troops to aid Valens after the Gothic revolt in AD 376 and it was Richomeres who led the army that fought the Goths at Ad Salices in AD 377. From AD 383 he was *Magister Militum Per Orientum* under Theodosius I and became a Consul in AD 384. Theodosius recalled him back to service in AD 388 to campaign with his nephew Arbogastes and the Generals Timasius and Promotus against the usurper Magnus Maximus who they subsequently defeated. From AD 388 Richomeres served as *Comes et Magister Utriusque Militiae* until his death on the way to give battle against his nephew Arbogastes who had seized power in the West. As noted above, Richomeres was in charge of the army at Ad Salices and therefore had a very good insight into how well a Gothic army defending a wagon laager could fight. He was with Gratian before the Battle of Adrianople as he was sent by Gratian with a letter telling Valens to await Gratian's arrival. He offered himself as a hostage to Fritigern at Adrianople when the tribune Aequitius refused to do so.

Richomeres was married to Ascyla and their son Theudemeres became King of the Franks. He was acquainted with Libanius who wrote several works concerning Richomeres.

Sebastianus

Place and date of birth unknown. Sebastianus was involved with the religious upheavals in Alexandria during AD 358, supporting Bishop George with expelling the adherents of Athanasius. He served as *Comes Rei Militaris* from AD 363 to AD 378, first under Julian before Julian's death and then under Valentinian I until his death in AD 374 and then under Gratian from AD 374 until Valens requested Gratian send him to take command of Valens' forces in AD 378, at this point he was promoted to *Magister Peditum*. Zosimus claims he went to Constantinople of his own accord due to the intrigues of the eunuchs of the Western court who had Gratian dismiss him from his command in the West. Valens further promoted him to command all his forces during the Gothic conflict of AD 378. He led a picked force of approximately 2,000 men against the Goths who had been plundering the region around Adrianople and surprised them in a night attack, leaving very few survivors and capturing so much loot that on his return to Adrianople he was forced to store some of it outside in the countryside. Perhaps due to this signal victory he persuaded Valens to launch an attack on Fritigern and the Goths making their way down towards Nike before the arrival of Gratian and his army and he perished along with Valens at the Battle of Adrianople. He too was acquainted with Libanius who wrote about him. Suda, using Eunapius, said this of Sebastianus:

Sebastianus. He lived during Valens' reign. During this reign there was a search for good soldiers, and this man was discovered, who exceeded all expectations since he had all the virtues. He fell short of none of his contemporaries and was justly compared even with the most highly and widely esteemed of the ancients. He loved war but refused to take risks, not for his own sake but for his men. He desired wealth only sufficient to equip him with excellent weapons. He preferred an austere and simple diet, enough to revive his strength but not enough to hinder him at the start of a task. Although he was exceedingly fond of his men, he did not pander to the troops, but erases all their eagerness to plunder the provincials and directed their rapacity against the enemy. Those who disobeyed these ordinances he punished severely, those who obeyed he helped to become wealthy. In a word, he himself was an exemplar of virtue. He held high and illustrious commands, but just as the Colossus of Rhodes, though striking because of its size, is not loved, so he, through an object of wonderment because of his lack of greed, did not inspire affection.

Victor

Place and date of birth unknown. He was a Sarmatian who attained high rank and status. First serving under Constantius II, upon that emperor's death in AD 360, he then served under Julian and accompanied him on his invasion of Sassanid Persia, acting as *Comes Rei Militaris*. Before Julian's death he was promoted to *Magister Peditum* and on Julian's death Jovian appeared to promote him to *Magister Equitum*. After the defeat of Procopius, and before the commencement of Valens' first Gothic war in AD 367, Victor was dispatched to the Goths to demand the reasons why they had supported Procopius' revolt. After the conclusion of that war in AD 369 he was sent with Arinthaeus to negotiate the terms of the treaty. He became a consul in AD 369. In AD 377 Valens sent him with Urbicius to the Sassanids to commence negotiations over Armenia but these were interrupted when he was recalled due to the on-going Gothic crisis. He was one of the high ranking officers consulted by Valens about what action to take before the Battle of Adrianople and Victor was one of those who counselled waiting for Gratian and his army. Having survived that battle he went to the West and was one of the first to inform Gratian of Valens' defeat. He travelled to Constantinople around AD 380 where he retired from active service.

He married the daughter of the Saracen Queen Mavia not long after the Battle of Adrianople. Like Richomeres and Sebastianus he was acquainted with Libanius who wrote about him. Ammianus said of him that although he was 'a Sarmartian by birth' he was 'foresighted and careful', qualities not usually associated with the Sarmartians!

The Goths

Athanaricus

Place and date of birth unknown. Athanaricus appears to have at one time been King of the Greuthungi Goths, because Ammianus calls him 'their most powerful ruler' when describing Valens' attack in AD 369. Yet later, Athanaricus is noted as being one of the Kings of the Tervingi Goths. Whatever the case may be, Athanaricus was the Gothic ruler whom Valens fought against in his Gothic campaigns from AD 367 to AD 369 and with whom he conducted the Treaty of AD 369 on the Danube. In the histories of Sozomen and Socrates they state that Athanaricus had a rival, Fritgern, and that a civil war broke out between the two. It may well be that there was a faction of the Goths, led by Fritigern, who were unhappy with the way that Athanaricus had conducted himself against Valens and as a result sided with Fritigern. Whatever the reasons, Fritgern appealed to the Romans for assistance and Valens sent a force stationed in Thrace to assist and as a result Athanaricus retreated with those Goths who remained faithful to him. There is some confusion in Zosimus' history as he sets this civil war after Adrianople, Theodosius I sending troops to aid Fritgern. As a result of this action by Fritgern, and Fritgern's conversion to Christianity, Athanaricus was stated as persecuting and putting to death Christians.

In AD 376 the Huns ravaged the territory of the Goths, defeating Athanaricus during a night assault and forcing him and his followers to seek refuge in the mountains bordering the old province of Dacia. He may have attempted to repair the old Roman frontier wall, the Limes Transalutanus, and use it as a defence against the Huns but he was attacked again by the Huns before the work was completed and he was forced once more to retreat. At this point many of his followers deserted him and headed for the perceived safety of the Roman Empire instead. Athanaricus decided on this course of action himself as he appeared on the banks of the Danube with his followers possibly accompanying Vithericus, King of the Greuthungi Goths, and the chieftains Alatheus, Saphrax and Farnobius. Athanaricus apparently remembered at this point that Valens may well have pointed out that Athanaricus told him he had taken a solemn oath never to enter Roman territory, hence his meeting Valens halfway on the Danube in AD 369, and as a result he led his remaining followers to the Carpathian mountains where Ammianus noted that Athanaricus had previously driven out the Sarmatians.

Athanaricus is next heard of seeking asylum within the Eastern Empire in January AD 381, where he was received very cordially, despite his previously being accused of persecuting Christian Goths. In fact, such was the esteem that Theodosius held him in that when Athanaricus died a short while after crossing into the Roman Empire he was buried with full honours due to a great king.

Fritigern

Place and date of birth unknown. The first we hear of Fritigern is when he made an appeal to Valens for support in the civil war between himself and Athanaricus. Valens' support gave Fritigern victory, and as a result both he and his followers converted to the Arian Christian faith. The next time we hear of him is when he arrived on the bank of the Danube in AD 376 with another Gothic chieftain called Alavivas, both apparently leading the Tervingi Goths. Fritigern and Alavivas sent envoys to Valens and he allowed them entry into Thrace, probably as a result of being given promises of Gothic warriors as auxiliaries, which would have greatly increased his Sassanid Persia expeditionary force, as well as cutting down on the expense of raising levies. However, the situation between the Goths and the Romans began to breakdown due to the inept treatment they were receiving. This led to open revolt when, as seen in Chapter 7, an attempt was made on both Fritgern and Alvivas' lives at a banquet given by the Roman Lupicinus.

Fritigern appears at this point to take control of most of the Tervingi on the Roman side of the Danube and for the next two years his Goths ravaged Thrace. It's not recorded whether he was leading the Goths at Ad Salices, but there is no reason to suppose not. It is doubtful he was the chieftain leading the Goths who made an attempt prior to the Battle of Adrianople at Constantinople itself, as recorded by Sozomen and I have discussed in a previous chapter. His most memorable act was leading the Goths to victory at Adrianople in AD 378. He appears to have led the Goths for several more years after the Battle of Adrianople, even making an attempt upon Constantinople, but is not heard of after AD 381, presumably due to his death.

Alatheus and Saphrax

Places and dates of birth unknown. The first we hear about these two chieftains is in Ammianus where after the suicide of the Greuthungi King Ermenrichus they took control of his young son Viderichus. We then next hear of them accompanying the Goths under Fritigern and it was the cavalry under both of their commands that was instrumental in the Roman defeat at Adrianople. We last hear of them in Zosimus where they accompany Fritigern again on his campaign against Athanaricus and forcing him to seek refuge in the Roman Empire. However, Zosimus' account conflicts with those of both Ammianus and Sozomen. It has been conjectured that Saphrax may have been of Hunnic origin due to his name.

Chapter Seventeen

The Sources

There are a number of ancient sources concerning Valens' Gothic wars and I have included here the more important surviving historical accounts, omitting those that are very brief or add nothing of value, such as that by Theodoret, Zonarius etc. Whilst some of these accounts are quite lengthy, they are important to the narrative, and are included here together for the first time.

Ammianus Marcellinus – Res Gestae Book XXXI (The Battle of Adrianople) But on the dawn of that day which is numbered in the calendar as the fifth before the Ides of August the army began its march with extreme haste, leaving all its baggage and packs near the walls of Hadrianopolis with a suitable guard of legions; for the treasury, and the insignia of imperial dignity besides, with the prefect and the emperor's council, were kept within the circuit of the walls. So after hastening a long distance over rough ground, while the hot day was advancing towards noon, finally at the eighth hour they saw the wagons of the enemy, which, as the report of the scouts had declared, were arranged in the form of a perfect circle. And while the barbarian soldiers, according to their custom, uttered savage and dismal howls, the Roman leader so drew up their line of battle that the cavalry on the right wing were first pushed forward, while the greater part of the infantry waited in reserve. But the left wing of the horsemen (which was formed with the greatest difficulty, since very many of them were still scattered along the roads) was hastening to the spot at swift pace. And while that same wing was being extended, still without interruption, the barbarians were terrified by the awful din, the hiss of whirring arrows and the menacing clash of shields; and since a part of their forces under Alatheus and Saphrax was far away and, though sent for, had not yet returned, they sent envoys to beg for peace. The emperor scorned these because of their low origin, demanding for the execution of a lasting treaty that suitable chieftains be sent; meanwhile the enemy purposely delayed, in order that during the pretended truce their cavalry might return, who, they hoped, would soon make their appearance; also that our soldiers might be exposed to the fiery summer heat and exhausted by their dry throats, while the broad plains gleamed with fires, which the enemy were feeding with wood and dry fuel, for this same purpose. To that evil was added another deadly one, namely, that men and beasts were tormented by severe hunger.

Meanwhile Fritigern, shrewd to foresee the future and fearing the uncertainty of war, on his own initiative sent one of his common soldiers as a herald, requesting that picked men of noble rank be sent to him at once as hostages and saying that he himself would fearlessly meet the threats of his soldiers and do what was necessary. The proposal of the dreaded leader was welcome and approved, and the tribune Aequitius, then marshal of the court and a relative of Valens, with the general consent was chosen to go speedily as a surety. When he objected, on the ground that he had once been captured by the enemy but had escaped from Dibaltum, and therefore feared their unreasonable anger, Richomeres voluntarily offered his own services and gladly promised to go, thinking this also to be a fine act and worthy of a brave man. And soon he was on his way [bringing] proofs of his rank and birth... As he was on his way to the enemy's rampart, the archers and the targeteers, then under the command of one Bacurius of Hiberia and Cassio, had rushed forward too eagerly in hot attack, and were already engaged with their adversaries; and as their charge had been untimely, so their retreat was cowardly; and thus they gave an unfavourable omen to the beginning of the battle. This unseasonable proceeding not only thwarted the prompt action of Richomeres, who was not allowed to go at all, but also the Gothic cavalry, returning with Alatheus and Saphrax, combined with a band of the Halani, dashed out as a thunderbolt does near high mountains, and threw into confusion all those whom they could find in the way of their swift onslaught, and quickly slew them.

On every side armour and weapons clashed, and Bellona, raging with more than usual madness for the destruction of the Romans, blew her lamentable war-trumpets; our soldiers who were giving way rallied, exchanging many encouraging shouts, but the battle, spreading like flames, filled their hearts with terror, as numbers of them were pierced by strokes of whirling spears and arrows. Then the lines dashed together like beaked ships, pushing each other back and forth in turn, and tossed about by alternate movements, like waves at sea.

And because the left wing, which had made its way as far as the very wagons, and would have gone farther if it had had any support, being deserted by the rest of the cavalry, was hard pressed by the enemy's numbers, it was crushed, and overwhelmed, as if by the downfall of a mighty rampart. The foot-soldiers thus stood unprotected, and their companies were so crowded together that hardly anyone could pull out his sword or draw back his arm. Because of clouds of dust the heavens could no longer be seen, and echoed with frightful cries. Hence the arrows whirling death from every side always found their mark with fatal effect, since they could not be seen beforehand nor guarded against. But when the barbarians, pouring forth in huge hordes, trampled down horse and man, and in the press of ranks no room for retreat could be gained anywhere, and the increased crowding left no opportunity for escape, our soldiers also, showing extreme contempt of falling in the fight, received their death-blows, yet struck down their assailants; and on both sides the strokes of axes split helmet and breastplate. Here one might see a barbarian filled with lofty courage, his cheeks contracted in a hiss, hamstrung or with right hand severed, or pierced through the side, on the very verge of death threateningly casting about his fierce glance; and by the fall of the combatants on both sides the plains were covered with the bodies of the slain strewn over the ground, while the groans of the dying and of those who had suffered deep wounds caused immense fear when they were heard. In this great tumult and confusion the infantry, exhausted by their efforts and the danger, when in turn strength and mind for planning anything were lacking, their lances for the most part broken by constant clashing, content to fight with drawn swords, plunged into the dense masses of the foe, regardless of their lives, seeing all around that every loophole of escape was lost. The ground covered with streams of blood whirled their slippery foothold from under them, so they could only strain every nerve to sell their lives dearly; and they opposed the onrushing foe with such great resolution that some fell by the weapons of their own comrades. Finally, when the whole scene was discoloured with the hue of dark blood, and wherever men turned their eyes heaps of slain met them, they trod upon the bodies of the dead without mercy. Now the sun had risen higher, and when it had finished its course through Leo, and was passing into the house of the heavenly Virgo, scorched the Romans, who were more and more exhausted by hunger and worn out by thirst, as well as distressed by the heavy burden of their armour. Finally our line was broken by the onrushing weight of the barbarians, and since that was the only resort in their last extremity, they took to their heels in disorder as best they could.

While all scattered in flight over unknown paths, the emperor, hedged about by dire terrors, and slowly treading over heaps of corpses, took refuge with the lancers and the Mattiarii, who, so long as the vast numbers of the enemy could be sustained, had stood unshaken with bodies firmly planted. On seeing him Trajanus cried that all hope was gone, unless the emperor, abandoned by his body-guard, should at least be protected by his foreign auxiliaries. On hearing this the general called Victor hastened to bring quickly to the emperor's aid the Batavi, who had been posted not far off as a reserve force; but when he could find none of them, he retired and went away. And in the same way Richomeres and Saturninus made their escape from danger.

And so the barbarians, their eyes blazing with frenzy, were pursuing our men, in whose veins the blood was chilled with numb horror: some fell without knowing who struck them down, others were buried beneath the mere weight of their assailants; some were slain by the sword of a comrade; for though they often rallied, there was no ground given, nor did anyone spare those who retreated. Besides all this, the roads were blocked by many who lay mortally wounded, lamenting the torment of their wounds; and with them also mounds of fallen horses filled the plains with corpses. To these ever irreparable losses, so costly to the Roman state, a night without the bright light of the moon put an end.

At the first coming of darkness the emperor, amid the common soldiers as was supposed (for no one asserted that he had seen him or been with him), fell mortally wounded by an arrow, and presently breathed his last breath; and he was never afterwards found anywhere. For since a few of the foe were active for long in the neighbourhood for the purpose of robbing the dead, no one of the fugitives or of the natives ventured to approach the spot.

The Caesar Decius, we are told, met a similar fate; for when he was fiercely fighting with the barbarians and his horse, whose excitement he could not restrain, stumbled and threw him, he fell into a marsh, from which he could not get out, nor could his body be found. Others say that Valens did not give up the ghost at once, but with his bodyguard and a few eunuchs was taken to a peasant's cottage near by, well fortified in its second storey; and while he was being treated by unskilful hands, he was surrounded by the enemy, who did not know who he was, but was saved from the shame of captivity. For while the pursuers were trying to break open the bolted doors, they were assailed with arrows from a balcony of the house; and fearing through the inevitable delay to lose the opportunity for pillage, they piled bundles of straw and firewood about the house, set fire to them, and burned it men and all. From it one of the bodyguards leaped through a window, but was taken by the enemy; when he told them what had happened, he filled them with sorrow at being cheated of great glory, in not having taken the ruler of the Roman Empire alive. This same young man, having later escaped and returned secretly to our army, gave this account of what had occurred. When Spain had been recovered, with a similar disaster the second of the Scipios, we are told, was burned with a tower in which he had taken refuge and which the enemy had set on fire. This much, at any rate, is certain, that neither Scipio nor Valens had the fortune of burial which is death's final honour.

Amid this manifold loss of distinguished men, the deaths of Trajanus and Sebastianus stood out. With them fell thirty-five tribunes, without special assignments, and leaders of bodies of troops, as well as Valerianus and Aequitius, the one having charge of the stables, the other, of the Palace. Among these also Potentius lost his life in the first flower of his youth; he was tribune of the promoti, respected by all good men and honoured both for his own services and those of his father Ursicinus, formerly a commander-in-chief. Certain it is that barely a third part of our army escaped. The annals record no such massacre of a battle except the one at Cannae, although the Romans more than once, deceived by trickery due to an adverse breeze of Fortune, yielded for a time to ill-success in their wars, and although the storied dirges of the Greeks have mourned over many a contest.

Paulus Orosius – The Seven Books of History against the Pagans Book VII

Now, in the thirteenth year of the reign of Valens, that is, a short time after Valens had carried on the destruction of the churches and the slaughter of the saints throughout the entire East, that root of our miseries all at once sent up very abundant shoots. For the race of the Huns, shut off for a long time by inaccessible mountains, stirred up by a sudden rage burst out against the Goths and drove them in widespread disorder from their old homes. The Goths, fleeing across the Danube, were received by Valens without the negotiation of any treaty and they did not even give over their arms to the Romans, by which trust could be placed in the barbarians with greater safety. Then, on account of the general, Maximus, driven by famine and injuries to rise in rebellion, they conquered the army of Valens and poured forth over all Thrace, mingling everything with slaughter, fire, and rapine. Valens, when, as he came out of Antioch, he was being dragged to his doom in an unfortunate war, stimulated by a late repentance for a very great sin, ordered the recall from exile of the bishops and other holy persons.

Thus, in the fifteenth year of his rule, Valens fought that lamentable war in Thrace with the Goths, who were then very well equipped with strong training and an abundance of resources. As soon as the squadrons of Roman cavalry were thrown into confusion by the sudden attack of the Goths, they left the companies of infantrymen without protection. Then the legions of infantry, becoming surrounded on all sides by the enemy's cavalry and, when first overwhelmed by showers of arrows and then mad with fear they were driven over devious paths, being completely cut to pieces by the swords and lances of those who were pursuing them, perished. The emperor himself, when wounded by an arrow and turned into flight he was carried into a house on a small farm and was concealed there, was caught by the pursuing enemy and was consumed by the fire that was set to the house, and that the testimony of his punishment and that of divine wrath might be a terrible example to posterity, he was even deprived of a common burial.

Socrates Scholasticus – Ecclesiastical History Book IV

The barbarians, dwelling beyond the Danube, called the Goths, having engaged in a civil war among themselves, were divided into two parties, one of which was headed by Fritigern, the other by Athanaric. When the latter had obtained an evident advantage over his rival, Fritigern had recourse to the Romans, and implored their assistance against his adversary. This was reported to the Emperor Valens, and he ordered the troops which were garrisoned in Thrace to assist those barbarians who had appealed to him against their more powerful countrymen; and by means of this subsidy they won a complete victory over Athanaric beyond the Danube, totally routing the enemy. This became the occasion for the conversion of many of the barbarians to the Christian religion: for Fritigern, to express his sense of the obligation the emperor had conferred upon him, embraced the religion of his benefactor, and urged those who were under his authority to do the same. Therefore it is that so many of the Goths are even to the present time infected with the errors of Arianism, they having on the occasion preferred to become adherents to that heresy on the emperor's account. Ulfilas, their bishop at that time, invented the Gothic letters, and translating the Sacred Scriptures into their own language, undertook to instruct these barbarians in the Divine oracles. And as Ulfilas did not restrict his labours to the subjects of Fritigern, but extended them to those who acknowledged the sway of Athanaric also, Athanaric regarding this as a violation of the privileges of the religion of his ancestors, subjected those who professed Christianity to severe punishments; so that many of the Arian Goths of that period became martyrs. Arius indeed, failing in his attempt to refute the opinion of Sabellius the Libyan, fell from the true faith, and asserted the Son of God to be 'a new God?': Deuteronomy 32:7 but the barbarians embracing Christianity with greater simplicity of mind despised the present life for the faith of Christ. With these remarks we shall close our notice of the Christianized Goths.

Not long after the barbarians had entered into a friendly alliance with one another, they were again vanquished by other barbarians, their neighbours, called the Huns; and being driven out of their own country, they fled into the territory of the Romans, offering to be subject to the emperor, and to execute whatever he should command them. When Valens was made acquainted with this, not having the least presentiment of the consequences, he ordered that the suppliants should be received with kindness; in this one instance alone showing himself compassionate. He therefore assigned them certain parts of Thrace for their habitation, deeming himself peculiarly fortunate in this matter: for he calculated that in future he should possess a ready and well-equipped army against all assailants; and hoped that the barbarians would be a more formidable guard to the frontiers of the empire even than the Romans themselves. For this reason he in the future neglected to recruit his army by Roman levies; and despising those veterans who had bravely straggled and subdued his enemies in former wars, he put a pecuniary value on the militia which the inhabitants of the provinces, village by village, had been accustomed to furnish, ordering the collectors of his tribute to demand eighty pieces of gold for every soldier, although he had never before lightened the public burdens. This change was the origin of many disasters to the Roman empire subsequently.

The barbarians having been put into possession of Thrace, and securely enjoying that Roman province, were unable to bear their good fortune with moderation; but committing hostile aggressions upon their benefactors, devastated all Thrace and the adjacent countries. When these proceedings came to the knowledge of Valens, he desisted from sending the adherents of the homoousion into banishment; and in great alarm left Antioch, and came to Constantinople, where also the persecution of the orthodox Christians was for the same reason come to an end. At the same time Euzoïus, bishop of the Arians at Antioch, departed this life, in the fifth consulate of Valens, and the first of Valentinian the younger; and Dorotheus was appointed in his place.

The Emperor Valens arrived at Constantinople on the 30th of May, in the sixth year of his own consulate, and the second of Valentinian the Younger, and found the people in a very dejected state of mind: for the barbarians, who had already desolated Thrace, were now laying waste the very suburbs of Constantinople, there being no adequate force at hand to resist them. But when they undertook to make near approaches, even to the walls of the city, the people became exceedingly troubled, and began to murmur against the emperor; accusing him of having brought on the enemy there, and then indolently prolonging the struggle there, instead of at once marching out against the barbarians. Moreover at the exhibition of the sports of the Hippodrome, all with one voice clamored against the emperor's negligence of the public affairs, crying out with great earnestness, 'Give us arms, and we ourselves will fight.' The emperor provoked at these seditious clamors, marched out of the city, on the 11th of June; threatening that if he returned, he would punish the citizens not only for their insolent reproaches, but for having previously favored the pretensions of the usurper Procopius; declaring also that he would utterly demolish their city, and cause the plough to pass over its ruins, he advanced against the barbarians, whom he routed with great slaughter, and pursued as far as Adrianople, a city of Thrace, situated on the frontiers of Macedonia. Having at that place again engaged the enemy, who had by this time rallied, he lost his life on the 9th of August, under the consulate just mentioned, and in the fourth year of the 289th Olympiad. Some have asserted that he was burnt to death in a village whither he had retired, which the barbarians assaulted and set on fire. But others affirm that having put off his imperial robe he ran into the midst of the main body of infantry; and that when the cavalry revolted and refused to engage, the infantry were surrounded by the barbarians, and completely destroyed in a body. Among these it is said the emperor fell, but could not be distinguished, in consequence of his not having on his imperial habit. He died in the fiftieth year of his age, having reigned in conjunction with his brother thirteen years, and three years after the death of the brother. This book therefore contains [the course of events during] the space of sixteen years.

After the Emperor Valens had thus lost his life, in a manner which has never been satisfactorily ascertained, the barbarians again approached the very walls of Constantinople, and laid waste the suburbs on every side of it. Whereat the people becoming indignant armed themselves with whatever weapons they could severally lay hands on, and sallied forth of their own accord against the enemy. The empress Dominica caused the same pay to be distributed out of the imperial treasury to such as volunteered to go out on this service, as was usually allowed to soldiers. A few Saracens also assisted the citizens, being confederates, who had been sent by Mavia their queen: the latter we have already mentioned. In this way the people having fought at this time, the barbarians retired to a great distance from the city.

Salaminius Hermias Sozomen – Ecclesiastical History Books VI–VII
For the Goths, who inhabited the regions beyond the Ister, and had conquered other barbarians, having been vanquished and driven from their country by the Huns, had passed over into the Roman boundaries.

The Huns, it is said, were unknown to the Thracians of the Ister and the Goths before this period; for though they were dwelling secretly near to one another, a lake of vast extent was between them, and the inhabitants on each side of the lake respectively imagined that their own country was situated at the extremity of the earth, and that there was nothing beyond them but the sea and water. It so happened, however, that an ox, tormented by insects, plunged into the lake, and was pursued by the herdsman; who, perceiving for the first time that the opposite bank was inhabited, made known the circumstance to his fellow-tribesmen. Some, however, relate that a stag was fleeing, and showed some of the hunters who were of the race of the Huns the way which was concealed superficially by the water. On arriving at the opposite bank, the hunters were struck with the beauty of the country, the serenity of the air, and the adaptedness for cultivation; and they reported what they had seen to their king. The Huns then made an attempt to attack the Goths with a few soldiers; but they afterwards raised a powerful army, conquered the Goths in battle, and took possession of their whole country. The vanquished nation, being pursued by their enemies, crossed over into the Roman territories. They passed over the river, and dispatched an embassy to the emperor, assuring him of their co-operation in any warfare in which he might engage, provided that he would assign a portion of land for them to inhabit. Ulphilas, the bishop of the nation, was the chief of the embassy. The object of his embassy was fully accomplished, and the Goths were permitted to take up their abode in Thrace. Soon after contentions broke out among them, which led to their division into two parts, one of which was headed by Athanaric, and the other by Fritigern. They took up arms against each other, and Fritigern was vanquished, and implored the assistance of the Romans. The emperor having commanded the troops in Thrace to assist and to ally with him, a second battle was fought, and Athanaric and his party were put to flight. In acknowledgment of the timely succor afforded by Valens, and in proof of his fidelity to the Romans, Fritigern embraced the religion of the emperor, and persuaded the barbarians over whom he ruled to follow his example. It does not, however, appear to me that this is the only reason that can be advanced to account for the Goths having retained, even to the present day, the tenets of Arianism. For Ulphilas, their bishop, originally held no opinions at variance with those of the Catholic Church;

for during the reign of Constantius, though he took part, as I am convinced, from thoughtlessness, at the council of Constantinople, in conjunction with Eudoxius and Acacius, yet he did not swerve from the doctrines of the Nicæan council. He afterwards, it appears, returned to Constantinople, and, it is said, entered into disputations on doctrinal topics with the chiefs of the Arian faction; and they promised to lay his requests before the emperor, and forward the object of his embassy, if he would conform to their opinions. Compelled by the urgency of the occasion, or, possibly, thinking that it was better to hold such views concerning the Divine nature, Ulphilas entered into communion with the Arians, and separated himself and his whole nation from all connection with the Catholic Church. For as he had instructed the Goths in the elements of religion, and through him they shared in a gentler mode of life, they placed the most implicit confidence in his directions, and were firmly convinced that he could neither do nor say anything that was evil. He had, in fact, given many signal proofs of the greatness of his virtue. He had exposed himself to innumerable perils in defence of the faith, during the period that the aforesaid barbarians were given to pagan worship. He taught them the use of letters, and translated the Sacred Scriptures into their own language. It was on this account, that the barbarians on the banks of the Ister followed the tenets of Arius. At the same period, there were many of the subjects of Fritigern who testified to Christ, and were martyred. Athanaric resented that his subjects had become Christian under the persuasion of Ulphilas; and because they had abandoned the cult of their fathers, he subjected many individuals to many punishments; some he put to death after they had been dragged before tribunals and had nobly confessed the doctrine, and others were slain without being permitted to utter a single word in their own defence. It is said that the officers appointed by Athanaric to execute his cruel mandates, caused a statue to be constructed, which they placed on a chariot, and had it conveyed to the tents of those who were suspected of having embraced Christianity, and who were therefore commanded to worship the statue and offer sacrifice; if they refused to do so, the men and the tents were burnt together. But I have heard that an outrage of still greater atrocity was perpetrated at this period. Many refused to obey those who were compelling them by force to sacrifice. Among them were men and women; of the latter some were leading their little children, others were nourishing their new-born infants at the breast; they fled to their church, which was a tent. The pagans set fire to it, and all were destroyed.

The Goths were not long in making peace among themselves; and in unreasonable excitement, they then began to ravage Thrace and to pillage the cities and villages. Valens, on inquiry, learned by experiment how great a mistake he had made; for he had calculated that the Goths would always be useful to the empire and formidable to its enemies, and had therefore neglected the reinforcement of the Roman ranks. He had taken gold from the cities and villages under the Romans, instead of the usual complement of men for the military service. On his expectation being thus frustrated, he quitted Antioch and hastened to Constantinople. Hence the persecution which he had been carrying on against Christians differing in opinion from himself, had a truce. Euzoïus, president of the Arians, died, and Dorotheus was proposed for his government.

Those in every city who maintained the Nicene doctrine now began to take courage, and more particularly the inhabitants of Alexandria in Egypt. Peter had returned there from Rome with a letter from Damasus, confirmatory of the tenets of Nicæa and of his own ordination; and he was installed in the government of the churches in the place of Lucius, who sailed away to Constantinople after his eviction. The Emperor Valens very naturally was so distracted by other affairs, that he had no leisure to attend to these transactions. He had no sooner arrived at Constantinople than he incurred the suspicion and hatred of the people. The barbarians were pillaging Thrace, and were even advancing to the very suburbs, and attempted to make an assault on the very walls, with no one to hinder them. The city was indignant at this inertness; and the people even charged the emperor with being a party to their attack, because he did not sally forth, but delayed offering battle. At length, when he was present at the sports of the Hippodrome, the people openly and loudly accused him of neglecting the affairs of the state, and demanded arms that they might fight in their own defence. Valens, offended at these reproaches, immediately undertook an expedition against the barbarians; but he threatened to punish the insolence of the people on his return, and also to take vengeance on them for having formerly supported the tyrant Procopius.

When Valens was on the point of departing from Constantinople, Isaac, a monk of great virtue, who feared no danger in the cause of God, presented himself before him, and addressed him in the following words: 'Give back, O emperor, to the orthodox, and to those who maintain the Nicene doctrines, the churches of which you have deprived them, and the victory will be yours.' The emperor was offended at this act of boldness, and commanded that Isaac should be arrested and kept in chains until his return, when he meant to bring him to justice for his temerity. Isaac, however, replied, 'You will not return unless you restore the churches.' And so in fact it came to pass. For when Valens marched out with his army, the Goths retreated while pursued. In his advances he passed by Thrace, and came to Adrianople. When at not great distance from the barbarians, he found them encamped in a secure position; and yet he had the rashness to attack them before he had arranged his own legions in proper order. His cavalry was dispersed, his infantry compelled to retreat; and, pursued by the enemy, he dismounted from his horse, and with a few attendants entered into a small house or tower, where he secreted himself. The barbarians were in full pursuit, and went beyond the tower, not suspecting that he had selected it for his place of concealment. As the last detachment of the barbarians was passing by the tower, the attendants of the emperor let fly a volley of arrows from their covert, which immediately led to the exclamation that Valens was concealed within the building. Those who were a little in advance heard this exclamation, and made known the news with a shout to those companions who were in advance of them; and thus the news was conveyed till it reached the detachments which were foremost in the pursuit. They returned, and encompassed the tower. They collected vast quantities of wood from the country around, which they piled up against the tower, and finally set fire to the mass. A wind which had happened to arise favored the progress of the conflagration; and in a short period the tower, with all that it contained, including the emperor and his attendants, was utterly destroyed. Valens was fifty years of age. He had reigned thirteen years conjointly with his brother, and three by himself.

Such was the fate of Valens. The barbarians, flushed with victory, overran Thrace, and advanced to the gates of Constantinople. In this emergency, a few of the confederate Saracens sent by Mavia, together with many of the populace, were of great service. It is reported that Dominica, wife of Valens, furnished money out of the public treasury, and some of the people, after hastily arming themselves, attacked the barbarians, and drove them from the city.

Zosimus – *Historia Nova* Book IV

After the death of Procopius, the emperor Valens sacrificed to his resentment the lives of many persons, and confiscated the property of many others. His intended expedition into Persia was obstructed by the incursions into the Roman territories of a Scythian tribe residing beyond the Ister. Against these he directed a competent force, arresting their progress and compelling them to surrender their arms. He sent them to several of his towns on the Ister, with orders for them to be kept in prison without chains.

These were the auxiliaries that were sent by a Scythian chief to Procopius. Their chief therefore demanding their dismissal from the emperor, on the ground that they had been sent at the request of ambassadors from the person who then held the sovereign authority, Valens refused to listen to this demand. He replied, that they had neither been sent for nor taken by him as friends, but as enemies. This produced a war with the Scythians. The emperor, perceiving that they designed to invade the Roman dominion, and were for that purpose collecting together with the utmost speed, drew up his army on the bank of the Ister. He himself was stationed at Marcianopolis, the largest city of Thrace, where he paid great attention to the discipline of the army, and to the supplies of provisions. He then appointed Auxonius prefect of the court, Sallustius having, by reason of his age, obtained permission to resign that office, which he had twice held. Auxonius, though on the eve of so dangerous a war, acted with the strictest justice in the collection of the tributes, being careful that no person was oppressed with exactions more than it was his right to pay. He likewise procured many transport-vessels, in which he conveyed provisions for the army through the Euxine Sea to the mouth of the Ister, and thence, that the army might be the more easily supplied, by boats to the several towns on the side of the river.

These transactions having taken place in the winter season, the emperor marched from Marcianopolis into the territory of the enemy, with the troops that were stationed near the Ister, and attacked the Barbarians. Not having sufficient resolution to come to a regular engagement, they took refuge in the marshes, from whence they occasionally sallied. The emperor therefore ordered his troops to continue at their stations, and collected all the slaves in the camp, and those who had the care of the baggage, promising a sum of money to every man who brought him the head of a Barbarian. This filled them with hopes of gaining the money, inducing them to go into the woods and fens, killing all they met, whose heads they brought to the emperor, and received the promised reward. By these means so many were destroyed that the rest petitioned for a truce. The emperor acceded to their entreaty, and a peace was concluded with them which reflected no dishonour on the Roman name. It was agreed, that the Romans should enjoy in security all. their former possessions, and that the Barbarians should not cross the river, nor enter into any part of the Roman dominions. Having concluded this treaty, the emperor returned to Constantinople, and the prefect of the court being dead, conferred that office on Modestus. He then prepared for the war with Persia.

While these affairs were so conducted, a barbarous nation, which till then had remained unknown, suddenly made its appearance, attacking the Scythians beyond the Ister. These were the Huns. It is doubtful whether they were Scythians, who lived under regal government, or the people whom Herodotus states to reside near the Ister, and describes as a weak people with flat noses, or whether they came into Europe from Asia. For I have met with, a tradition, which relates that the Cimmerian Bosphorus was rendered firm land by mud brought down the Tanais, by which they were originally afforded a land-passage from Asia into Europe. However this might be, they, with their wives, children, horses, and carriages, invaded the Scythians who resided on the Ister; and though they were not capable of fighting on foot, nor understood in what, manner even to walk, since they could not fix their feet firmly on the ground, but live perpetually, and even sleep, on horseback, yet by the rapidity with which they wheeled about their horses, by the suddenness of their excursions and retreat, shooting as they rode, they occasioned great slaughter among the Scythians. In this they were so incessant, that the surviving Scythians were compelled to leave their habitations to these Huns, and crossing the Ister, to supplicate the emperor to receive them, on their promise to adhere to him as faithful soldiers. The officers of the fortified towns near the Ister deferred complying with this petition, until they should learn the pleasure of the emperor, who permitted them to be received without their arms. The tribunes and other officers therefore went over to bring the Barbarians unarmed into the Roman territory; but occupied themselves solely in the gratification of their brutal appetites, or in procuring slaves, neglecting every thing that related to public affairs. A considerable number therefore crossed over with their arms, through this negligence. These, on arriving into the Roman dominion, forgot both their petition and their oaths. Thus all Thrace, Pannonia, and the whole country as far as Macedon and Thessaly were filled with Barbarians, who pillaged all in their way.

Of these extreme dangers the emperor was informed by messengers, who were purposely sent to him. Having then arranged his affairs in Persia in the best possible manner, he hastened from Antioch to Constantinople; and from thence marched into Thrace against the fugitive Scythians. On his route a remarkable spectacle presented itself. The body of a man was lying in the road, perfectly motionless, which appeared as if it had been whipped from head to foot; the eyes wore open, and gazed on all who approached it. Having enquired of him, who he was, and from whence he came, and who had so severely beat him, and receiving no reply, they concluded it to be a prodigy, and shewed him to the emperor as he passed by. Although he made the same enquiries, it still remained speechless, and though void of motion and apparently dead, yet the eyes appeared as if alive. At length it suddenly disappeared. The spectators were unable to account for the prodigy; but persons who were skilled in such events, said that it portended the future state of the empire; that the commonwealth should appear as if it had been beaten and whipped, until, by the misconduct of its magistrates and ministers, it would expire. If we take all circumstances into consideration, this interpretation will indeed appear just.

The emperor Valens, perceiving that the Scythians were pillaging Thrace, resolved to send the troops who had accompanied him from the east, and who were expert horsemen, to make the first charge on the Scythian horse. These having therefore received orders from the emperor, left Constantinople in small detachments, and killing the straggling Scythians with their spears, brought many of their heads into the city every day. As the fleetness of their horses, and the force of their spears, caused the Scythians to suppose it difficult to overcome these Saracens, they attempted to circumvent them by stratagem. They planted in several places ambuscades of three Scythians to one Saracen; but their design was rendered abortive, as the Saracens by means of the swiftness of their horses could easily escape whenever they perceived any considerable number approaching. The Saracens with their spears committed such ravage among the Scythians, that at length despairing of success, they preferred passing the Ister and surrendering themselves to the Huns, than being destroyed by the Saracens. When they had retired from all the places near Constantinople, the emperor had room to draw out his army. He was now hesitating how to manage the war, so great a multitude of Barbarians being at hand, and was tormented by the ill conduct of his own officers. He was notwithstanding afraid of discharging them under such turbulent circumstances, and was likewise doubtful whom to appoint in their place, since no one appeared who was capable of such employments. At this juncture, Sebastianus arrived at Constantinople from the west, although the emperors there, by reason of their youth, were unacquainted with affairs, and attended to little beside the calumnies of the eunuchs who waited on them. Upon hearing of his arrival, Valens, knowing his ability both in civil and military affairs, appointed him to the command of his army, and entrusted him with the whole management of the war. Sebastianus, observing the indolence and effeminacy both of the tribunes and soldiers, and that all they had been taught was only how to fly, and to have desires more suitable to women than to men, requested no more than two thousand men of his own choice. He well knew the difficulty of commanding a multitude of ill-disciplined dissolute men, and that a small number might more easily be reclaimed from their effeminacy; and, moreover, that it was better to risk a few than all. By these arguments having prevailed upon the emperor, he obtained his desire. He selected, not such as had been trained to cowardice and accustomed to flight, but strong and active men who had lately been taken into the army, and who appeared to him, who was able to judge of men, to be capable of any service. He immediately made trial of each of them, and obviated their defects by continual exercise; bestowing commendations and rewards on all who were obedient, but appearing severe and inexorable to those who neglected their duty. Having by these means infused into them the principles of the military art, he took possession of several fortified towns, for the security of his army. From these he frequently surprised the Barbarians as they came out for forage. Sometimes, when they were loaded with spoils, he killed them and took what they carried; at other times he destroyed them when they were intoxicated or washing themselves in the river.

When he had by these methods cut off great part of the Barbarians, and the remainder felt such dread of him that they dared not attempt to forage, an extraordinary degree of envy was excited against him. From this envy proceeded hatred; until at length the court eunuchs, at the instigation of those who had lost their command, accused him to the emperor, who by these means was induced to entertain unjust suspicions of him. Sebastianus sent a request to the emperor, desiring him to remain where he then was, and not to advance; since it was not easy to bring such a multitude to a regular engagement. He, moreover, observed that it would be better to protract the war in harassing them by ambuscades, until they should be reduced to despair from the want of necessaries, and rather than expose themselves to the misery and destruction of famine, either surrender themselves, or depart from the Roman territory and submit to the Huns. While he gave the emperor this counsel, his adversaries persuaded him to march forward with his whole army; that the Barbarians were almost destroyed, and the emperor might gain a victory without trouble. Their counsel, though the least prudent, so far prevailed, that the emperor led forth his whole army without order. The Barbarians resolutely opposed them, and gained so signal a victory, that they slew all, except a few with whom the emperor fled into an unfortified village. The Barbarians, therefore, surrounded the place with a quantity of wood, which they set on fire. All who had fled thither, together with the inhabitants, were consumed in the flames, and in such a manner, that the body of the emperor could never be found. When the affairs of the empire were reduced to this low condition, Victor, who commanded the Roman cavalry, escaping the danger with some of his troops, entered Macedon and Thessaly. From thence he proceeded into Moesia and Pannonia, and informed Gratian, who was then in that quarter, of what had occurred, and of the loss of the emperor and his army. Gratian received the intelligence without uneasiness, and was little grieved at the death of his uncle, a disagreement having existed between them. Finding himself unable to manage affairs, Thrace being ravaged by the Barbarians, as were likewise

Pannonia and Moesia, and the towns upon the Rhine being infested by the neighbouring Barbarians without controul, he chose for his associate in the empire, Theodosius, who was a native of a town called Cauca, in the part of Spain called Hispania Callaecia, and who possessed great knowledge and experience of military affairs. Having given him the government of Thrace and the eastern provinces, Gratian himself proceeded to the west of Gaul, in order, if possible, to compose affairs in that quarter.

Jordanes – The Origins and Deeds of the Goths Books XXV–XXVI

But after a short space of time, as Orosius relates, the race of the Huns, fiercer than ferocity itself, flamed forth against the Goths. We learn from old traditions that their origin was as follows: Filimer, king of the Goths, son of Gadaric the Great, who was the fifth in succession to hold the rule of the Getae after their departure from the island of Scandza – and who, as we have said, entered the land of Scythia with his tribe – found among his people certain witches, whom he called in his native tongue Haliurunnae. Suspecting these women, he expelled them from the midst of his race and compelled them to wander in solitary exile afar from his army. There the unclean spirits, who beheld them as they wandered through the wilderness, bestowed their embraces upon them and begat this savage race, which dwelt at first in the swamps, – a stunted, foul and puny tribe, scarcely human, and having no language save one which bore but slight resemblance to human speech. Such was the descent of the Huns who came to the country of the Goths.

This cruel tribe, as Priscus the historian relates, settled on the farther bank of the Maeotic swamp. They were fond of hunting and had no skill in any other art. After they had grown to a nation, they disturbed the peace of neighboring races by theft and rapine. At one time, while hunters of their tribe were as usual seeking for game on the farthest edge of Maeotis, they saw a doe unexpectedly appear to their sight and enter the swamp, acting as guide of the way; now advancing and again standing still. The hunters followed and crossed on foot the Maeotic swamp, which they had supposed was impassable as the sea. Presently the unknown land of Scythia disclosed itself and the doe disappeared. Now in my opinion the evil spirits, from whom the Huns are descended, did this from envy of the Scythians. And the

Huns, who had been wholly ignorant that there was another world beyond Maeotis, were now filled with admiration for the Scythian land. As they were quick of mind, they believed that this path, utterly unknown to any age of the past, had been divinely revealed to them. They returned to their tribe, told them what had happened, praised Scythia and persuaded the people to hasten thither along the way they had found by the guidance of the doe. As many as they captured, when they thus entered Scythia for the first time, they sacrificed to Victory. The remainder they conquered and made subject to themselves. Like a whirlwind of nations they swept across the great swamp and at once fell upon the Alpidzuri, Alcildzuri, Itimari, Tuncarsi and Boisci, who bordered on that part of Scythia. The Alani also, who were their equals in battle, but unlike them in civilization, manners and appearance, they exhausted by their incessant attacks and subdued. For by the terror of their features they inspired great fear in those whom perhaps they did not really surpass in war. They made their foes flee in horror because their swarthy aspect was fearful, and they had, if I may call it so, a sort of shapeless lump, not a head, with pin-holes rather than eyes. Their hardihood is evident in their wild appearance, and they are beings who are cruel to their children on the very day they are born. For they cut the cheeks of the males with a sword, so that before they receive the nourishment of milk they must learn to endure wounds. Hence they grow old beardless and their young men are without comeliness, because a face furrowed by the sword spoils by its scars the natural beauty of a beard. They are short in stature, quick in bodily movement, alert horsemen, broad shouldered, ready in the use of bow and arrow, and have firm-set necks which are ever erect in pride. Though they live in the form of men, they have the cruelty of wild beasts.

When the Getae beheld this active race that had invaded many nations, they took fright and consulted with their king how they might escape from such a foe. Now although Hermanaric, king of the Goths, was the conqueror of many tribes, as we have said above, yet while he was deliberating on this invasion of the Huns, the treacherous tribe of the Rosomoni, who at that time were among those who owed him their homage, took this chance to catch him unawares. For when the king had given orders that a certain woman of the tribe I have mentioned, Sunilda by name, should be bound to wild horses and torn apart by driving them at full speed in opposite directions (for he was roused to fury by her husband's treachery to him), her brothers Sarus and Ammius came to avenge their sister's death and plunged a sword into Hermanaric's side. Enfeebled by this blow, he dragged out a miserable existence in bodily weakness. Balamber, king of the Huns, took advantage of his ill health to move an army into the country of the Ostrogoths, from whom the Visigoths had already separated because of some dispute. Meanwhile Hermanaric, who was unable to endure either the pain of his wound or the inroads of the Huns, died full of days at the great age of one hundred and ten years. The fact of his death enabled the Huns to prevail over those Goths who, as we have said, dwelt in the East and were called Ostrogoths.

The Visigoths, who were their other allies and inhabitants of the western country, were terrified as their kinsmen had been, and knew not how to plan for safety against the race of the Huns. After long deliberation by common consent they finally sent ambassadors into Romania to the Emperor Valens, brother of Valentinian, the elder Emperor, to say that if he would give them part of Thrace or Moesia to keep, they would submit themselves to his laws and commands. That he might have greater confidence in them, they promised to become Christians, if he would give them teachers who spoke their language. When Valens learned this, he gladly and promptly granted what he had himself intended to ask. He received the Getae into the region of Moesia and placed them there as a wall of defence for his kingdom against other tribes. And since at that time the Emperor Valens, who was infected with the Arian perfidy, had closed all the churches of our party, he sent as preachers to them those who favored his sect. They came and straightway filled a rude and ignorant people with the poison of their heresy. Thus the Emperor Valens made the Visigoths Arians rather than Christians. Moreover, from the love they bore them, they preached the gospel both to the Ostrogoths and to their kinsmen the Gepidae, teaching them to reverence this heresy, and they invited all people of their speech everywhere to attach themselves to this sect. They themselves as we have said, crossed the Danube and settled Dacia Ripensis, Moesia and Thrace by permission of the Emperor.

Soon famine and want came upon them, as often happens to a people not yet well settled in a country. Their princes and the leaders who ruled them in place of kings, that is Fritigern, Alatheus and Safrac, began to lament

the plight of their army and begged Lupicinus and Maximus, the Roman
commanders, to open a market. But to what will not the 'cursed lust for
gold' compel men to assent? The generals, swayed by avarice, sold them at
a high price not only the flesh of sheep and oxen, but even the carcasses
of dogs and unclean animals, so that a slave would be bartered for a loaf
of bread or ten pounds of meat. When their goods and chattels failed, the
greedy trader demanded their sons in return for the necessities of life. And
the parents consented even to this, in order to provide for the safety of their
children, arguing that it was better to lose liberty than life; and indeed it is
better that one be sold, if he will be mercifully fed, than that he should be
kept free only to die.

Now it came to pass in that troublious time that Lupicinus, the Roman
general, invited Fritigern, a chieftain of the Goths, to a feast and, as the event
revealed, devised a plot against him. But Fritigern, thinking no evil, came
to the feast with a few followers. While he was dining in the praetorium he
heard the dying cries of his ill-fated men, for, by order of the general, the
soldiers were slaying his companions who were shut up in another part of
the house. The loud cries of the dying fell upon ears already suspicious,
and Fritigern at once perceived the treacherous trick. He drew his sword
and with great courage dashed quickly from the banqueting-hall, rescued
his men from their threatening doom and incited them to slay the Romans.
Thus these valiant men gained the chance they had longed for--to be free
to die in battle rather than to perish of hunger--and immediately took arms
to kill the generals Lupicinus and Maximus. Thus that day put an end to
the famine of the Goths and the safety of the Romans, for the Goths no
longer as strangers and pilgrims, but as citizens and lords, began to rule the
inhabitants and to hold in their own right all the northern country as far as
the Danube.

When the Emperor Valens heard of this at Antioch, he made ready an
army at once and set out for the country of Thrace. Here a grievous battle
took place and the Goths prevailed. The Emperor himself was wounded and
fled to a farm near Hadrianople. The Goths, not knowing that an emperor
lay hidden in so poor a hut, set fire to it (as is customary in dealing with a
cruel foe), and thus he was cremated in royal splendor. Plainly it was a direct
judgment of God that he should be burned with fire by the very men whom

he had perfidiously led astray when they sought the true faith, turning them aside from the flame of love into the fire of hell. From this time the Visigoths, in consequence of their glorious victory, possessed Thrace and Dacia Ripensis as if it were their native land.

Abbreviations

Amm – Ammianus Marcellinus
Anon. Val. – Anonymus Valesianus Pt1
Aur. Vic. – Aurelius Victor
Claud. – Claudian
SHA – *Scriptores Historiae Augustae*
Jord. – Jordanes
Pang. Lit. – *Panegyrici Latini*
Soc. – Socrates Scholasticus
Soz. – Salaminius Hermias Sozomen
Zon. – Zonaras
Zos. – Zosimus

Notes

Chapter 1

1. Wolfram, *History of the Goths* pp. 98–99.
2. Procopius, *The Gothic Wars*.
3. The drawings of the Column of Theodosius are to be found in the Musee du Louvre, Cabinet des Dessins. The drawings by Mathieu Lorichs and others of the Column of Arcadius are in Trinity College, Cambridge, Department of Drawings, Copenhagen and the Bibliotheqe Nationale, Paris. They can also be found in *Barbarians And Bishops: Army, Church, and State in the Age of Arcadius and Chrysostom*, Liebeschuetz (1990), and can also be found on the internet.
4. Amm BkXXXI, 2, 18.
5. McLynn, p. 53–56. Bigger wagons could be used pulled by as many as eight oxen (Miller & Firman p. 71).
6. McLynn, p. 423.
7. Ibid p. 55.
8. Claudian stated that the Goths during the fifth century began to use ditch and bank defences to protect their settlements, very similar to that of their Roman counterparts. This was likely down to the Goths in Roman service bringing back knowledge of field defences when they returned to their settlements on leave.
9. The surviving fragments of the Gothic Bible consist of codices containing a large part of the New Testament and some parts of the Old Testament that were written down from the original text during the sixth to eighth century AD.
10. During the third century AD the Goths were not only able to take cities by storm but also by besieging them. They appeared to have had the use not only of scaling ladders but other siege equipment, possibly siege engines, as well. By the fourth century they appear to have lost both the knowledge of the use of siege engines and also the siege engines themselves as at Adrianople they only had the use of hastily made scaling ladders when attempting to storm that city after the Battle of Adrianople.
11. Unruh (1993).

Chapter 2

1. Kulikowski, (2007) p.18.
2. Amm BkXXXI, 5, 15–17; Jord. BkXVI–XVIII; Zon. BkXII, 20; Zos. BkI, 22–24.
3. Amm BkXXXI, 5, 15; Zos. BkI, 24–36.
4. Zos. BkI, 37.
5. Aur. Vic. 33; Europius BkIV, VIII; SHA Vita Valerians 1–3, Vita Gallieni V–VI, XIII; Jord BkXX; Zon BkXII, 21–25; Zos. BkI, 37–40.

6. SHA Div. Claud VI-XI; Zos. BkI, 42.

7. Zos. BkI, 43.

8. Aur. Vic. 33; SHA Div. Claud. XI-XII; Zon. BkXII, 26; Zos. BkI, 46.

9. SHA Div. Aurel XXX (Aurelian was noted as being acclaimed as Gothicus); Zos. BkI, 48–56.

10. Aur. Vic. 35; SHA Div. Aurel XXXVII; Zon. BkXII, 27; Zos. BkI, 62.

11. Aur. Vic. 36; SHA Vita Tacitus XIII; Zon. BkXII, 28; Zos. BkI, 63.

12. Aur. Vic. 37; SHA Vita Probi; Zon. BkXII, 29; Zos. BkI, 64–71.

13. Aur. Vic. 38; SHA Vita Carus; Zon. BkXII, 30.

14. Aur. Vic. 39; Zon. BkXII, 30.

15. Aur. Vic. 39; Zon. BkXII, 31.

16. Pang. Lit. 8(5) & 11(3).

17. Vegetius BkI, 17.

18. Pang. Lit. 10(2).

19. Anon. Val. 5, 27; Zos. BkII, 15–28.

20. Zos. BkII, 21.

21. Zosimus claimed that a Gothic tribe, the Thaiphalians (Taifali) sent 500 cavalry against Constantine and his army and routed him. Zos. BkII, 31.

22. Although this victory is attributed to Constantine, it was actually his son Constantius, later to become Constantius II, who took the field against the Goths. Constantius had been acclaimed 'Gothicus' (CIL 3705) at some stage and this must have been prior to when Ammianus' surviving histories begins, AD 354, as Ammianus does not mention Constantius embarking on any campaigns against the Goths, nor did Julian or any of the other surviving histories. Zonaras stated that the Goths were joined by the Sarmatians and Constantine defeated both of those tribes in Thrace (Zon. BkXIII, 21).

23. Jord. BkXXI.

24. Ibid BkXXII.

25. Ibid BkXXIII.

26. Anon. Val. 5, 31–32; Aur. Vic. 41, 13; Eutropius BkX, VII; Festus BkXXVI;

27. Amm BkXVII, 13, 19–20. Ammianus also recorded that Constantius II had 'asked the Scythians for auxiliaries, either for pay or as a favour' in the winter of AD 360 (Amm BkXX, 8, 1). This may be the same approach that Libanius recorded (Libanius Oration XII, 62).

28. Constantius had been accused of murdering large numbers of his family after Constantine's death and whilst there is scant proof of this, the death of Gallus would have further cemented suspicions against Constantius. It would be much better if Julian were to be seen to have died a noble death in battle than to increase resentment against Constantius even further!

29. Amm BkXX, 4, 12–21; Zos. BkIII, 9. Julian had penned several panegyrics to Constantius, *The Heroic Deeds of Constantius* and *In Honour of the Emperor Constantius*. The tone of these works indicated that Julian had at one time held his uncle with some esteem, if not affection.

30. Amm BkXXI, 16, 18–19.

31. Amm BkXXIII, 3, 4–5. Julian divided his invasion army into two parts and sent 30,000 northward towards Armenia under Procopius and Sebastianus, where they would then launch another attack upon the Sassanids. It's highly doubtful Julian would have handed over more than half of his troops to those two generals and this must have meant the rest of the army under his command was at least 30,000 strong.
32. Amm BkXXIII, 2, 7; Zos. BkIII, 26. Libanius was obviously bending the truth when he claimed Julian had not hired Gothic auxiliaries or raised large armies (Libanius Oration XVIII, 169).
33. Amm BkXXV, 3–23; Zon BkXIII; Zos. BkIII, 29.
34. Amm BkXXV, 5, 4–9; Eutropius BkX, XVII–XVIII; Zos. BkIII, 30–36. See Chapter 3 for the accession of Valentinian and Valens.

Chapter 3
1. Amm BkXXVI, 4, 4; Zos. BkIV, 1.
2. Amm BkXXVI, 5, 1–6; Soz. BkVI, 6; Zon. BkXIII, 15, 130; Zos. BkIV, 2.
3. Amm BkXXVI, 4, 5–6.
4. Amm BkXXVI, 5, 7; Zos. BkIV, 3.
5. Amm BkXXVI, 8–14; Soc BkIV, III. However, see Zos. BkIV, 4–6 for a different perspective on this.
6. Amm XXIII, 3, 2; Amm BkXXVI, 6, 2; Zos. BkIV, 4.
7. Amm BkXXVI, 6, 11; Zos. BkIV, 7.
8. Amm BkXXVI, 6, 12–13. The two legions were probably the two Palatine legions by that name that appear in the *Notitia Dignitatum*, an official document dated between AD 395 and AD 420 that listed the various units of the Late Roman army and the field armies and commands they were attached to and where those units were stationed.
9. Amm BkXXVI, 10, 3.
10. Zos. BkIV, 7.
11. Amm BkXXVI, 7, 11–12.
12. Amm BkXXVI, 7, 13–17, Amm BkXXVI, 8, 1–5; Zos. BkIV, 7.
13. Amm BkXXVI, 8, 6–15.
14. Amm BkXXVI, 9, 1–11; Soc BkIV, V; Zos. BkIV, 8. Sozomen's account of Procopius' death was far more graphic! (Soz. BkVI, 8), Zonaras gives a very similar account to that of Sozomen's (Zon. BkXIII, 16, 140).
15. Amm BkXXVI, 10, 1–5.

Chapter 4
1. Amm BkXXVII, 5, 1; Zos. BkIV, 10.
2. Amm BkXXVII, 5, 2.
3. Ibid BkXXVII, 5, 5.
4. Ibid BkXXVII, 5, 5.
5. Ibid BkXXVII, 5, 6. Although Ammianus called Athanaricus the 'most powerful ruler' of the Greuthungi Goths, he was later to become the ruler of the Tervingi

Goths, as was discussed in Chapter Five. How this situation came about is unknown.

6. Amm BkXXVII, 5, 6. However Zosimus does not record a battle between Valens and Athanaricus and gives a different account of the Roman campaign and the defeat of the Goths (Zos. BkIV, 10–11).
7. Amm BkXXVII, 5, 7–9; Them Or 10 (in Heather & Matthews 1991).
8. Amm BkXXVII, 5, 9; Zos. BkIV, 11; Them Or 10.

Chapter 5

1. Soc. Bk4, 33.
2. Soc. Bk4, 33.
3. Amm BkVII, 5, 10; Soc BkIV, 33; Soz. BkVI, 37. Jordanes also appeared to indicate that the Goths' conversion to Christianity happened after they had crossed the Danube in AD 376 (Jord. BkXXV).
4. Heather, (1996) p. 98; 2005 pp. 146–150; Thompson (1996), pp. 1–2, pp. 13,14.
5. Jord. BkXXIV.
6. Amm BkXXXI, 2, 1–2.
7. Thompson (1996) Chapter 3.
8. Amm BkXXXI, 3, 2.
9. Ibid BkXXXI, 3, 3.
10. Ibid BkXXXI, 3, 3.
11. Ibid BkXXXI, 3, 4–6.
12. Ibid BkXXXI, 3, 7–8.
13. Heather, (2006) *The Fall of the Roman Empire* p. 152.
14. Amm BkXXXI, 3, 8.
15. Amm BkXXXI, 3, 8; Soc. Bk34; Soz. BkVI, 37; Zos. BkIV, 20.

Chapter 6

1. Amm BkXXVII, 8, 1.
2. Ibid BkXXVII, 8, 2, Amm BkXXVII, 8, 5.
3. Amm BkXXVII, 8, 3.
4. Amm BkXXVII, 8, 6–7.
5. Amm BkXXVII, 8, 7–10.
6. Amm BkXXVII, 9, 1–2, Amm BkXXVIII, 6, 1–4.
7. Ibid BkXXVIII, 2, 11–14.
8. Amm XIV, 2, 1–20.
9. Amm XXVII, 9, 6. Ammianus used Diogmiae to describe a scratch force made up of armed citizens, infantry that were lightly armed for such operations were generally called *expediti*.
10. Amm BkXXVII, 9, 7. Zosimus placed the Isaurian incursion to after the death of Valentinian (Zos. BkIV, 20).
11. Ibid BkXXVII, 10, 1–2.
12. Ibid BkXXVII, 10, 3–4.

13. Ibid BkXXVII, 10, 6–16; Zosimus appeared to claim that Valentinian was in fact defeated at Solicinium (Zos. BkIV, 9).
14. Amm BkXXVIII, 2, 1–4.
15. Ibid BkXXVII, 12, 1–3.
16. Ibid BkXXVII, 12, 4–8.
17. Ibid BkXXVII, 12, 10.
18. Ibid BkXXVII, 12, 11–12.
19. Ibid Bk XXVII, 12. 13–14.
20. Ibid BkXXVII, 12, 15.
21. Ibid BkXXVII, 12, 16.
22. Ibid BkXXVII, 12, 16–18.
23. Ibid BkXXVIII, 5, 1.
24. Ibid BkXXVIII, 5, 2.
25. Ibid BkXXVIII, 5, 3–4.
26. Ibid BkXXVIII 5, 5–7.
27. Ibid BkXXVIII, 5, 8–11.
28. Ibid BkXXVIII, 5, 12–13.
29. Ibid BkXXVIII, 5, 13–15.
30. Amm BkXXVIII, 1, 1–57. Valentinian was forced to rescind the decree after being petitioned by a group of ex-Prefects and Governors (Amm XXVIII, 1, 24–25).
31. Ibid BkXXVIII, 1, 28.
32. Ibid BkXXVIII, 1, 57.
33. Ibid BkXXIX, 1, 1–3; Zos. BkIV, 13.
34. Ibid BkXXIX, 1, 4.
35. Ibid BkXXIX, 1, 16.
36. Amm BkXXIX, 1, 18–44; Amm BkXXIX, 2, 1–20.
37. Ibid BkXXIX, 3, 1–9.
38. Ibid BkXXIX, 4, 2.
39. Ibid BkXXIX, 4, 2–7.
40. Ibid BkXXIX, 5, 1–2.
41. Ibid BkXXIX, 5, 3–5.
42. Ibid BkXXIX, 5, 6–8.
43. Ibid BkXXIX, 5, 9.
44. Ibid BkXXIX, 5, 10–12.
45. Ibid BkXXIX, 5, 13–14.
46. Ibid BkXXIX, 5, 15–16.
47. Ibid BkXXIX, 5, 17–18.
48. Ibid BkXXIX, 5, 19–24.
49. Ibid BkXXIX 5, 25–27.
50. Ibid BkXXIX, 5, 28–30.
51. Ibid BkXXIX, 5, 31–35.
52. Ibid BkXXIX, 5, 36–40.
53. Ibid BkXXIX, 5, 41.
54. Ibid BkXXIX, 5, 41–44.

55. Ibid XXIX, 5, 45–50.
56. Amm BkXXIX, 5, 51–55. Zosimus only briefly mentioned the revolt of Firmus (Zos. BkIV, 16).
57. Amm BkXVII, 12, 8–17
58. Amm BkXXIX, 6, 1–3. Zosimus called Maximinus' son Celestius (Zos. BkIV, 16).
59. Amm BkXXIX, 6, 5.
60. Ibid BkXXIX, 6. 6–7.
61. Ibid BkXXIX, 6, 8–14.
62. Ibid BkXXIX, 6, 15–16; Zos. BkIV, 16.
63. Amm BkXXX, 1, 1–3.
64. Ibid BkXXX, 1, 4.
65. Ibid BkXXX, 1, 5–7.
66. Ibid BkXXX, 1, 8–15.
67. Ibid BkXXX, 1, 16–23.
68. Amm BkXXX, 3, 1–7, Zos. BkIV, 16 may allude to the treaty between Valentinian and Macrianus.
69. Amm BkXXX, 5, 1–2.
70. Ibid BkXXX, 5, 3–10.
71. Ibid BkXXX, 5, 11–13.
72. Ibid BkXXX, 5, 4–18.
73. Amm BkXXX, 6; 1–6; Soc. Bk IV, 31; Soz. BkVI, 36; Zos. IV, 17. Zonaras' text is clearly wrong at this point as he claimed Valentinian died of old age! (Zon. BkXIII, 15, 133).
74. Amm BkXXX, 10, 1–6.

Chapter 7

1. Amm BkXXXI, 1, 1–5; Zos. BkIV, 18. Zonaras recorded a different version of that inscription (Zon. BkXIII, 16, 140).
2. Amm BkXXXI, 4, 1; Jord. Bk XXV; Soc. BKIV, 34; Soz. BkVI, 38; Zos. BkIV, 20.
3. Amm BkXXXI, 4, 2–4.
4. Ibid BkXXXI, 4, 5.
5. Ibid BkXXXI, 4, 6–11.
6. Ibid BkXXXI, 4, 12–13.
7. Ibid BkXXXI, 4, 13.
8. Amm BkXXXI, 5, 1–3; Zos. BkIV, 20.
9. Amm BkXXXI, 5, 4.
10. AMM BkXXXI, 5, 5–9; Jord. BkXXVI.
11. Amm BkXXXI, 6, 1–3.
12. Ibid BkXXXI, 6, 3–4.
13. Ibid BkXXXI, 6, 5–8.

Chapter 8

1. Amm BkXXXI, 7, 1.
2. Ibid BkXXXI, 7, 2–3.
3. Ibid BkXXXI, 7, 4.

4. Ibid BkXXXI, 7, 5.
5. Ibid BkXXXI, 7, 6–7.
6. Ibid BkXXXI, 8–9.
7. Amm XXXI, 7, 10–11. The Barritus may have originally been introduced into the Roman army by Germanic recruits. The sound would have been enhanced by the troops holding their shields in front of their faces, the concavity of the shields then increasing the volume of the war cry. The troops also clashed their spears against the shields, creating an even more menacing noise. See also Vegetius BkIII, 18.
8. Ibid BkXXXI, 7, 12.
9. Ibid BkXXXI, 7, 13–14. Ammianus was able to draw upon his own battlefield experiences to describe the horror a Roman soldier faced during combat.
10. Amm BkXXXI, 7, 15–16, Amm BkXXXI, 8, 1.
11. Ibid BkXXXI, 8, 2–3.

Chapter 9

1. Amm BkXXXI, 8, 2–3.
2. Ibid BkXXXI, 8, 4–7.
3. Ibid BkXXXI, 8, 7–10. This incident may be where Aequitius claims to have been captured, and then made his escape from Dibaltum. If so it is surprising that Ammianus does not mention Aequitius being present or his capture there.
4. Ibid BkXXXI, 9, 1–5.
5. Ibid BkXXX, 2, 1–3.
6. Ibid BkXXX, 2, 4–6.
7. Ibid BkXXX, 2, 6. As discussed in Chapter Fifteen, a typical field army size was approximately 25,000. If Valens intended invading with three armies as was claimed by Ammianus then the invasion force would have numbered at least 75,000. Julian's invasion army was probably at least 50–60,000 strong.
8. Amm BkXXX, 2, 6–8.
9. Ibid BkXXXI, 10, 1–4.
10. Ibid BkXXXI, 10, 5.
11. Ibid BkXXXI, 10, 6–10.
12. Ibid BkXXXI, 10, 11–22.
13. Ibid BkXXXI, 11, 1; Soc. BkIV, 38; Soz. BkVI, 39.
14. Amm BkXXXI, 11, 1, Zos. BkIV, 22–23.
15. Ibid BkXXXI, 11. 1–2.
16. Amm BkXXXI, 11, 2; Zosimus stated that 2.000 men in total were chosen by Sebastianus, this general then trained this force to battle readiness (Zos. BkIV, 23).
17. Amm BkXXXI, 11, 3–5. Zosimus exaggerated Sebastianus' exploits, and even claimed he captured 'walled cities'!
18. Amm BkXXXI, 11, 5.
19. Ibid BkXXXI, 11, 6.

Chapter 10

1. Amm BkXXXI, 12, 1.
2. Amm BkXXXI, 12, 1; Zos. BkIV, 23–24.

3. Amm BkXXXI, 12, 2–3.
4. Ibid BkXXXI, 12, 3.
5. Ibid BkXXXI, 12, 4.
6. Ibid BkXXXI, 12, 4–5.
7. Ibid BkXXXI, 11, 6.
8. Amm BkXXXI, 12, 5–6. Zosimus claimed that it was in fact Sebastianus who counselled Valens not to attack the Goths, urging him to instead wear down the Goths through a combination of 'manoeuvres and ambushes until, weakened by a lack of provisions, they either surrendered or retreated from Roman territory, preferring to give themselves up to the Huns rather than suffer the pitiful destruction usually resulting from a famine' (Zos. BkIV, 23).
9. Amm BkXXXI 12, 7.
10. Ibid BkXXXI, 12, 8–9.

Chapter 11

1. Barbero, (2008); Burns, (1973, 1994, 2003); Donnelly, (2013); Eisenberg, (2009); Lenski, (2002); McDowell, (2001).
2. The most obvious accounts of armies defeating much larger ones would be Alexander defeating Darios' army at Gaugamela, and Julian defeating the Alamanni at Argentoratum.
3. Zos. 4, 24.
4. Heather, (2005), p. 105.
5. Amm BkXXXI, 12, 11.
6. Vegetius BkIII, 6.
7. Ammianus recorded that the Romans would show their willingness to fight by clashing their weapons against their shields and raising their famous war cry, the Barritus.
8. See above 'notes' for Chapter Nine, footnote 3.
9. Orosius, Socrates and Sozomen all claimed that it was the Roman cavalry on the right flank who fled the battlefield first, and their actions were the ultimate cause of the Roman defeat.
10. Amm BkXVI, 12, 38–41.
11. Vegetius BkII, 15 details the arms and armour of the infantrymen of the legion which may well be that of the troops when he wrote between AD 390 and AD 420. BkII, 17 has the troops forming 'a wall of iron'. Ammianus describes a number of battles where the Romans locked shields and formed a wall. See also Rance, (2004).
12. Vegetius BkIII, 18.
13. Zos. BkIV, 9. Amm BkXXVII, 1, 6 may also relate to this incident.
14. Amm BkXXXI, 13, 14–16; Jord. BkXXVI; Orosius BkVII; Soc. BkIV 38; Soz. BkVI, 40; Zon. BkXII, 139; Zos. BkIV, 24.

Chapter 12

1. Amm BkXXXI, 15, 3.
2. Ibid XXXI, 15, 4–5.

3. Ibid XXXI 15, 5–6.
4. Ibid XXXI, 15, 7–9.
5. Ibid XXXI, 15, 9–15.
6. Ibid BkXXXI, 16, 1.
7. Zos. BkIV, 24.
8. Amm BkXXXI, 16, 2; Zos. BkIV, 25.
9. Amm XXXI, 16, 2.
10. Amm BkXXXI, 16, 3; Libanius Or 24, 15.
11. Amm XXXI, 16, 4.
12. Amm XXXI, 16, 5; Soc. BkV, 1; Soz. BkVII, 1. Zos. (BkIV, 22–23) differs in that he stated that the Saracens had arrived in Constantinople before Valens left that city to travel to Melanthias, and that they attacked the Goths at that time. This directly conflicts with the other accounts and it is probably the case that Zosimus was once more getting his history muddled up as I have related in other chapters.
13. Amm BkXXXI, 16, 7.
14. Amm BkXXXI, 16, 8; Zos. BkIV, 26.
15. It became difficult to recruit for the army after Adrianople and The Theodosian Code details what measures were taken by Theodosius to ensure that not only the 'right' kind of recruits were selected, but also ways of preventing the draft, Theodosian Code 7, 13, 8–11.
16. See Lenski, (1997).

Chapter 15

1. See Lenski, (2002).
2. Vegetius BkII, 7–14.
3. See MacMullen, Appendix A.
4. See Coello (1996). The Perge Fragments, dated from the reign of Anastasius, detail the pay rates and numbers of troops in a legion. Unfortunately the information on these numbers has to date not been released yet by Professor Fatih Onur.
5. Vegetius claimed that the legion up to the reign of Diocletian was 6,000 men strong (BkI & BkII). If Diocletion doubled the number of legions and Auxilia units by dividing each unit into two then this would make each new legion 3,000 men strong and each Auxilia unit 500 men strong. For actual unit sizes see Coello.
6. The Batavi and Heruli Auxila Palatina units were brigaded together and when they did so they appeared to have shared the same standards (Amm BkXXVII, 1, 6). Whether the Lanciarii and the Mattiarii legions also shared the same standards when they were brigaded together is not known.
7. Vegetius BkII, 15.
8. The pen & ink drawings of the Column of Theodosius are in the Musee du Louvre, Cabinet des Dessins. They can be downloaded from the internet. The drawings by Mathieu Lorichs and others of the Column of Arcadius are in Trinity College, Cambridge, Department of Drawings, Copenhagen and the Bibliotheqe Nationale, Paris. These drawings can be found in *Barbarians And Bishops: Army, Church, and Stae in the Age of Arcadius and Chrysostom*, Liebeschuetz (2004).

Bibliography

The internet has been both a curse and a godsend to the researcher the last ten years. Many journals and other academic works can be found using an internet search engine. Whole libraries of books can be sourced, some for free, others for a small sum as electronic books and many of those books and translations I have listed below can be found on the internet. Some of the translations are inferior works, written by those with a basic or imperfect grasp of the ancient language they are translating from, or they are very old works, long out of copyright that have been superseded by far superior translations. Whilst I have consulted material that can be found in electronic form, I am still a person who prefers the feel and look of a real book.

Primary Sources

Anonymous *Scriptores Historiae Augusta*, Leob in three volumes, translated by David Magie (1921–1932).

Jordanes, *The Origin and Deeds of the Goths* translated by C C Mierow (1908).

Libanius, *Orations*, Loeb in three volumes, translated by A F Norman (1969–1977).

Marcellinus Ammianus, *Res Gestae*, Loeb in three volumes, translated by J C Rolfe (1935–1940).

Orosius Paulus, *The Seven Books of History Against the Pagans* translated by R J Deferrari (1964).

Salaminius Hermias Sozomen *The Ecclesiastical History* translated by E Walford (1888).

Scholasticus Socrates, *The Ecclesiastical History* translated by E Walford (1888).

Themistius, *Oration 10* translated by Heather (1991).

Vegetius, *Epitome of Military Science* translated by N P Milner (1995).

Victor Aurelius, *De Caesaribus*: translated by H W Bird, 1994.

Zonarius *History* translated by T M Banchich and E N Lane (2009).

Zosimus, *Historia Nova* translated by R T Ridley (2004).

Secondary Sources

Agier M, *On the Margins of the World: The Refugee Experience Today* (Cambridge, 2008).

Allfree, J B, Cairns J, Carey, B T, *Warfare in the Ancient World* (Barnsley, 2005).

Barbero A, *The Day of the Barbarians: The Battle That Led to the Fall of the Roman Empire* (New York, 2008).

Bishop M C, Coulston J C, *Roman Military Equipment from the Punic Wars to the Fall of Rome* (London, 2005).

Blockley R C, *East Roman Foreign Policy: Formation and Conduct from Diocletian to Anastasius* (Leeds, 1992).

Blockley R C, *The Fragmentary Classicising Historians of the Later Roman Empire: Eunapius, Olympiodorus, Priscus and Malchus* (1981).

Bowerstock G W, Brown P, Grabar O (Editors), *Late Antiquity: A Guide to the Postclassical World* (London, 1999).

Bowman A, Cameron A, Garnsey P (Editors), *The Cambridge Ancient History Volume 12: The Crisis of Empire, AD 193–337* (Cambridge, 2005).

Burns T S, *Barbarians Within The Gates of Rome: A Study of Roman Military Policy And The Barbarians, CA. 375–425 A.D.* (Bloomington, 1994).

Burns T S, *Rome And The Barbarians, 100B.C.- A.D.400* (London, 2003).

Burns T S, *The Battle of Adrianople: A Reconsideration* Historia 22 pp. 336–45 (1973).

Cameron A, Garnsey P (Editors), *The Cambridge Ancient History, Vol. 13: The Late Empire, AD 337–425* (Cambridge, 2003).

Coello T, *Unit Sizes in the Late Roman Army*, British Archaeological Reports (BAR) International 645 (1996).

Christie N, *From the Danube to the Po: the Defence of Pannonia and Italy in the Fourth and Fifth Centuries AD*, Proceedings of the British Academy 141, pp. 547–578 (2007).

Cromwell R S, *The Rise and Decline of the Late Roman Field Army* (Shippensburg, 2002).

Delbruck H, *The Barbarian Invasions* (Lincoln, 1990).

Dixon K R, Southern P, *The Late Roman Army* (London, 2000).

Donnelly P, *What Happened at Adrianople?* Web-based article (2013).

Drivers J W, Hunt D, 1999 *The Late Roman World and Its Historian: Interpreting Ammianus Marcellinus* (London, 1999).

Eisenberg R, *The Battle of Adrianople: A Reappraisal* Hirundo Vol.8, pp. 108–120 (2009).

Elton H, *Warfare in Roman Europe AD 350–425* (Oxford, 1996).

Erdkamp P (Editor), *A Companion to the Roman Army* (Oxford, 2001).

Errington R M, *Roman Imperial Policy: From Julian to Theodosius* (Chapel Hill, 2006).

Ferrill A, *The Fall of the Roman Empire: The Military Explanation* (London, 1988).

Gibbon E 1988 *The History of the Decline and Fall of the Roman Empire*, London

Gilliver C M, Goldsworthy A, Whitby M, *Rome at War: 58 BC–AD 696* (Oxford, 2005).

Goldsworthy A, *Roman Warfare* (London, 2000).

Goldsworthy A, *The Complete Roman Army* (London, 2003).

Goldsworthy A, *The Fall Of The West: The Death Of The Roman Superpower* (London, 2009).

Grant M, *The Roman Emperors: A Biographical Guide To The Rulers of Imperial Rome, 31 BC–AD 476* (London, 1985).

Grant M, *The Fall of the Roman Empire* (London, 1997).

Halsall G, *Barbarian Migrations and the Roman West, 376–568* (Cambridge, 2009).

Harries J, *Imperial Rome AD 284 to 363: The New Empire* (Edinburgh, 2012).

Hazlitt W, 'The Classical Gazetteer: A Dictionary of Ancient Sites' (London, 1851).

Heather P, *Empires And Barbarians: Migration, Development And The Birth Of Europe* (London, 2009).

Heather P, *Goths And Romans* pp. 332–489, (Oxford, 1991).

Heather P, Matthews J, *The Goths in the Fourth Century* (Liverpool, 1991).

Heather P, *The Huns and the End of the Roman Empire in Western Europe* (1995), 'The English Historical Review', Vol 110, No. 435, pp. 4–41.

Heather P, *The Goths*, (Oxford, 1996).

Heather P, *The Fall Of The Roman Empire: A New History* (London, 2005).

Heather P, *Goths in the Roman Balkans c.350–500* (2007), 'Proceedings of the British Academy', 141, pp. 163–190.

Jones A H M, *The Later Roman Empire 284–602 Vols I & II* (Oxford, 1973).

Jones A H M, Martindale J R, Morris J (Editors), *The Prosopography Of The Later Roman Empire* (Cambridge, 2006).

Kelly C, *Ruling the Later Roman Empire* London, 2004).

Kulikowski M, *Rome's Gothic Wars* (Cambridge, 2007).

Liebeschuetz J H W G, *The Lower Danube Region under Pressure: from Valens to Heraclius* (2007), 'Proceedings of the British Academy', 141, pp. 101–134.

Lee A D, *Information and Frontiers: Roman Foreign Relations in Late Antiquity* (Cambridge, 2006).

Lee A D, *War In Late Antiquity: A Social History* (Oxford, 2007).

Lee A D, *From Rome to Byzantium AD 363 to 565: The Transformation of Ancient Rome* (Edinburgh, 2013).

Lenski N, *Initium mali Romano imperio: Contemporary Reactions to the Battle of Adrianople* (1997), 'Transactions of the American Philological Association', 127, p. 129–168.

Lenski N, *Failure of Empire: Valens and the Roman State in the Fourth Century A.D.* (London, 2002).

MacDowall S, *Twilight of the Empire: The Roman Infantryman 3rd to 6th Century AD* (Oxford, 1994).

MacDowell S, *Adrianople AD 378: The Goths crush Rome's legions* (Oxford, 2001).

MacMullen R, *Corruption And The Decline Of Rome* (London, 1988).

Matthews J, *Western Aristocracies And Imperial Court AD 364–425* (Oxford, 1998).

Matthews J, *The Roman Empire of Ammianus* (London, 2008).

McLynn F, *Wagons West: The Epic Story of America's Overland Trails* (London, 2003).

Miller J, Firman S G, *Overland in a Covered Wagon: An Autobiography* (London, 1931).

Nicasie M J, *Twilight of Empire: The Roman army from the reign of Diocletian until the battle of Adrianople* (Amsterdam, 1998).

Nixon C E V, Rodgers B A, *In Praise of Later Roman Emperors: The Panegyrici Latini* (Oxford, 1994).

Norwich J J, *Byzantium: The Early Centuries* (London, 1988).

Parker H M D, *The Legions of Diocletian and Constantine*, 'The Journal of Roman Studies', Vol 23, pp. 175–189 (1933).

Peddie J, *The Roman War Machine* (Stroud, 2004).

Pharr C, (Trans.) *The Theodosian Code And Novels And The Simondian Constitutions* (New Jersey, 2001).

Potter D S, *A Companion to the Roman Empire* (Oxford, 2009).

Potter D S, *The Roman Empire at Bay, AD 180–395* (London, 2004).

Rance P, *The Fulcum, the Late Roman and Byzantine Testudo: the Germanization of Roman Infantry Tactics?* 'Greek, Roman and Byzantine Studies', 44, pp. 265–326 (2004).

Rohrabacher D, *The Historians of Late Antiquity* (London, 2002).

Runkel F, *Die Schlacht bei Adrianopel* (Rostock, 1903).

Sabin P, Whitby M, Van Wees H (Editors), *The Cambridge History of Greek and Roman Warfare: Rome from the Late Republic to the Late Empire* (Cambridge, 2007).

Santosuosso A, *Storming The Heavens: Soldiers, Emperors And Civilians In The Roman Empire* (London, 2004).

Speidel M P, *Raising New Units for the Late Roman Army : Auxilia Palatina*, (1996), 'Dumbarton Oaks Papers', Vol 50, pp. 163–170.

Stephenson I, *Romano-Byzantine Infantry Equipment* (Stroud, 2006).

Stephenson P, *Constantine: Unconquered Emperor, Christian Victor* (London, 2009).

Thompson E A, (Trans.) *A Roman Reformer And Inventor: Being A New Text Of The Treatise De Rebus Bellicis* (Oxford, 1952).

Thompson E A, *The Huns* (Oxford, 1996).

Unruh J D, *The Plains Across: The Overland Emigrants and the Trans-Mississippi West, 1840–60* (Chicago, 1993).

Wacher J, (Editor), *The Roman World* (London, 1990).

Wheeler E L, *The legion as a phalanx* (Chiron, 1979), pp. 303–318.

Whitby M, *Rome at War AD 293–696* (Oxford, 2002).

Whitby M, 2007 *The Late Roman Army and the Defence of the Balkans* (2007), 'Proceedings of the British Academy', 141, pp. 135–161.

Williams S, *Diocletian and the Roman Recovery* (London, 1997).

Wolfram H, *History Of The Goths* (London, 1990).

Wolfram H, *The Roman Empire and Its Germanic Peoples* (London, 1997).

Index